Layered Cloth

The Art of Fabric Manipulation

Ann Small

SEARCH PRESS

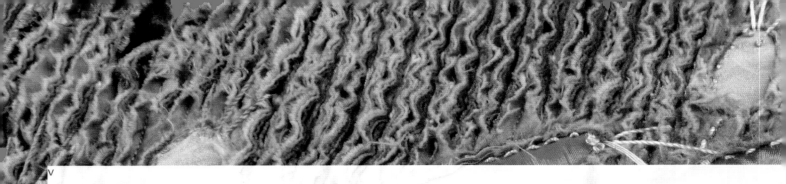

v

ACKNOWLEDGEMENTS

Thanks to Charlotte Pryor for the kind loan of *Natural Drama*.

To my husband Ian, who has always been prepared to chauffeur me anywhere to follow my textile pursuits.

To Roz Dace for her initial encouragement to write a book.

To Edward Ralph, my patient editor, and all the staff at Search Press, who made me feel so welcome.

Lastly to Paul Bricknell for bringing my work alive on the printed page.

First published in 2017

Search Press Limited
Wellwood, North Farm Road,
Tunbridge Wells, Kent TN2 3DR

Illustrations and text copyright © Ann Small 2017

Photographs by Paul Bricknell at Search Press Studios

Photographs and design copyright © Search Press Ltd 2017

ISBN: 978-1-78221-334-5

The Publishers and author can accept no responsibility for any consequences arising from the information, advice or instructions given in this publication.

Suppliers
If you have difficulty in obtaining any of the materials and equipment mentioned in this book, then please visit the Search Press website for details of suppliers:
searchpress.com

You are invited to visit the author's website:
asmalldesign.co.uk

Printed in China through Asia Pacific Offset

Front cover
From Rags to Riches
This joyful textile piece is the result of playing with colour. I was looking for interesting combinations and contrasts in hue. The scraps of fabric that make it up were placed with complete disregard for how they joined. As a result, when the surface was slashed or cut away, it revealed the exciting mismatched and raw edges of the cloth beneath the surface. The ragged scraps thus become a rich and invigorated cloth.

Page 1
Birds in Flight
It is surprising what you can come up with when you begin to play the fabric manipulation game: these birds emerged while I was making a spiral twist for another project – the shape brought a beak to mind, so I continued manipulating the fabric until these characterful birds emerged. They are displayed with the aid of a skeletonised umbrella. Each one is tied to a spoke, ensuring that they are comfortably spaced out and relatively easy to display at exhibition – time is of the essence on set-up day!

Pages 2–3
Natural Drama
Weather, however fleeting, can be a great source of inspiration. This piece was inspired by clouds gathering over a field of luminous yellow rapeseed in full bloom. The result is dramatic, not just because of the contrast in colours the scudding clouds provided as they swept across the countryside, but because of the scale and relative proportions in which the colours appear. At times nature demonstrates the true possibilities of colour, pushing all of our colour theory to its limits.

These pages
An Old Master
Wonderful inspiration can be gleaned from an Old Master's paintings. Optical colour mixing can be done with fabrics just as it does in paint. Vincent Van Gogh is a particular favourite of mine. His brush strokes suggest slashing and stitching and his inventive use of colour is to be revered.

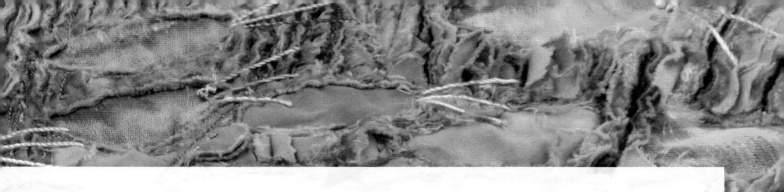

Contents

Introduction

Colour, texture and design have always been at the core of my creative work and I find working with cloth a particular fascination and pleasure. I played about a great deal with fabric when I was a young mum, creating costumes for my three daughters' dance performances. This led on to making costumes for others, which gradually developed into a full-time business making and hiring out costumes. Although this was lucrative for me, I much preferred the making to the hiring and washing, so as a result I sold up. It was quite a wrench selling my costumes themed around *Snow White and the Seven Dwarfs*, each of which had its own cloth sculpture mask!

I then took up the study of making authentic historical costume and embroidery, and spent several wonderful years passing my craft on to others. My favourite technique then was reverse appliqué, which involves stacking several layers of fabric, sewing a grid through them, then cutting through in places to reveal the colours beneath. I believe I passed my enthusiasm for this technique to many of my students and while doing so discovered endless potential variations within the design, particularly with the juxtaposition of colours.

This book shows how to combine some of my favourite techniques to form impressive textile artworks of considerable richness and variety, all of which are dynamic and vibrant. Coloured fabrics are stacked, sewn together in places, and then cut. The cutting disturbs the surface tension which allows the buried cloth to surface and the colours to mix in the eye.

I hope that as you work your way through this book, you will create a personal portfolio of samples and designs, leading on to creating your own style and artistic applications.

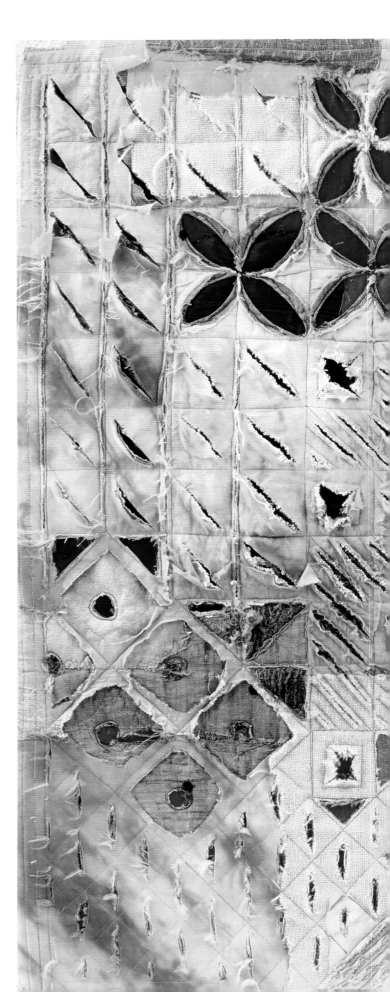

Celebration of Colour

Although there appear to be a lot of colours used in this piece, it was worked in just three carefully considered layers: the bottom layer is a mixture of reds, plums and aubergines; the middle layer various purples, mauves and violets; and the top layer is constructed of yellows and oranges.

Tools and materials

Two of the most important choices to make for the techniques described in this book are the cloth and scissors you use. I suggest you buy the best equipment you can afford. Cheap scissors in particular are a waste of time and money.

The fabrics you use can be new or recycled. For large projects, I recommend new cotton poplin. Dying the fabric yourself will give you more control of the colours.

Scissors

Cutting through multiple layers of fabric will quickly dull the scissors, so I like to buy a new pair after making two large projects, then demote the old ones to other jobs. I always mark new pairs of scissors with the date so I know which pair are the sharpest.

Sprung shears Your hands work really hard with the layering techniques so I suggest you use a new sharp pair of 20cm (8in) and 12.5cm (5in) sprung shears for the slashing. Unlike scissors, sprung shears spring open automatically after every cut, which helps to reduce hand strain.

Medium-sized scissors Reserve a nice sharp pair of scissors for cutting the fabrics before layering.

Medium-sized embroidery scissors Extra sharp pointed scissors are good for snipping threads and for tackling tiny fiddly areas in the slashing process.

Paper scissors Cutting paper will quickly blunt your fabric scissors. Keep an old pair of old scissors to use for cutting the paper patterns.

Seam ripper These tiny tools, used to cut the fabric between parallel sewn lines, are useful but need to be handled with caution. It is all too easy to get carried away and find yourself cutting right through to the base fabric by mistake. To use them, poke the sharp end though the fabric to the required depth and push to cut a small hole. Remove the sharp end from the hole and put the little red button end in instead, then tear. This will help to prevent digging too deep into the fabric stack.

TIP
It is tempting to use tiny embroidery scissors or even hardanger scissors for the slashing. These are too lightweight: the work of cutting through lots of layers means that they will not last long.

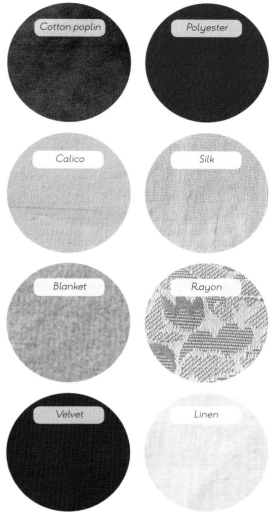

Cotton poplin
Polyester
Calico
Silk
Blanket
Rayon
Velvet
Linen

Fabric

Many different fabrics can be used for these versatile techniques. Those coloured on both sides tend to be best, as the finished textile artwork will show both sides of a fabric. Printed fabric can be used although the reverse side may be a bit dull. Thicker fabrics are useful as a base fabric. Whatever you choose, your fabrics should be prewashed to allow for shrinkage and colour transfer. This is especially important when using fabric you have dyed yourself. Having said all this, I encourage you to experiment with different fabrics in your samples. You may come up with a unique effect.

Cotton poplin This is the fabric I prefer to use for most of my layered work. It is a close-weave fabric which is not inclined to fray. When used in cut layers it does not 'clog' together as other fabrics can; instead it tends to flick open like the pages of a book. It also takes dyes well. Most other lightweight natural and synthetic fabrics will work and can be used mixed alongside the poplin.

Viscose, rayon, linen, wool, cotton and silk These are other good choices of fabric that work well with the layering technique. Knitted fabrics like jersey (t-shirt material) and satin viscose make a nice rolled edge when cut. White t-shirt fabric will dye well too.

Felted fabric Old blanket, or wool garments that have felted in the washing machine, are useful fabrics to use in order to add some volume and height to the stack without being too stiff.

Fusible interfacing This can be used instead of paper for applying the design. I prefer to use Stayflex interfacing. This is woven, which means it remains flexible and does not alter the characteristics of the fabric as much as non-woven interfacing.

DIFFICULT TYPES OF FABRIC

The following fabrics can be used, but they require additional thought and planning.
*When used in a stack, **calico** will tend to clog and stick to the adjacent layers.*
*Using only **silk** leaves a very flat finished result that does not demonstrate the technique to best effect.*
*Stiff **polyesters** and **acetates** will not allow the layer beneath to fluff up or 'bloom', but they can be used effectively at the base of a stack.*
***Cotton velvet** and **corduroy** are generally too bulky to use except sparingly.*

Sewing materials

Threads

A small selection of different coloured machine threads in cotton or viscose will be needed for the techniques in this book. You can also use machine embroidery thread which is finer. Multicoloured thread is also useful.

As the techniques mostly involve working from the back of the stacks, the machine thread colour will come from the bobbin, so I suggest you prepare several bobbins with the colours of fabric you are using so that you do not need to stop while working. The techniques featured are fairly robust in style, so several weights of embroidery threads can be used from stranded cotton to thicker threads – even crochet cotton and wool can be used for embellishment.

I suggest you avoid metallic thread. It is more fragile than other threads, and will likely cause problems with snapping when sewing through multiple layers. In addition, a fine metallic thread can looks overly-delicate and out of place with the robust style of the layered fabric. This is, of course, my personal preference and if you really like the effect then you may choose to experiment with metallic threads. For the best results with metallic thread, select a large machine needle – size 90 or 100 (US 14 or 16) – or use it in the bobbin only. The large eye and the large punched hole will mitigate the problems listed above to some extent.

For the designs in this book, machine stitching is mostly used for the functional purpose of holding the fabrics together, rather than for decoration or embellishment. However, as with my note on metallic threads above, if you can make it work for you, then go ahead. Experimentation is key to the technique.

Hand sewing needles

A mixed pack of hand sewing needles will likely provide all you need. There is no need to obsess about which needle to use, as it ultimately boils down to using one that you find comfortable to use for the task at hand. With that said, for general hand stitching I use crewel or embroidery needles

in sizes 3–9, plus a size 22 chenille needle. Chenille needles have a larger eye, which makes them particularly useful when working with thicker thread.

A size 8 sewing needle is a good start for the hand sewing work in this book, but feel free to use a larger or smaller gauge if you prefer. Whatever sort of needle you choose, it must glide comfortably through the fabric and have a large enough hole to thread easily. Invest in a needle threader, as it saves time and frustration. I recommend a chenille needle, as it has a large eye which will take the thicker embellishing threads. Its length means it is also comfortable for hand-sewing through multiple layers. A thicker sharp chenille needle, such as a Prym size 16 or 18, is useful for embellishing the layered cloth with thicker embroidery threads.

Hand sewing needles

A selection of different threads for use with both hand and machine sewing.

Sewing machine

A machine that will work simple electric straight stitch is all that is necessary. If your machine will also work zig-zag or other decorative stitches, all the better.

It can be confusing choosing a new machine so here are a few things to know before you go to buy:

• Electric machines with computerised controls provide you with a vast array of features. Useful features to look for include: up–down needle position, lock stitch, and automatic buttonhole.

• The lock stitch feature will lock the threads at the beginning and end of a line which will secure the stitches when we start the slashing.

• Electric machines with manual controls are cheaper but tend to have a smaller stitch selection, and more limited width and length controls.

• Make sure to enquire about the price of various attachments – some makes of machine charge a lot more than others for similar features.

• A moveable needle position is useful and this is usually activated from the width button. The centre position is used throughout this book unless otherwise stated.

• A machine with adjustable pressure foot height will make your work a lot easier when sewing through thick fabrics or layers.

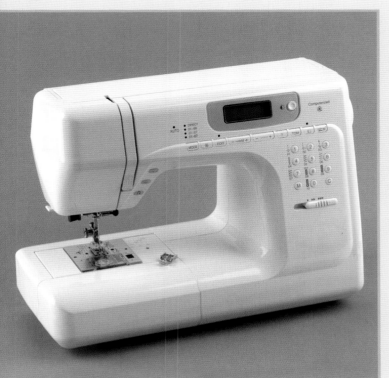

TIP

Consider carefully if you actually need a machine to connect to your computer or lots of automatic patterns. These are fun if your budget allows, but not necessary.

Machine feet

The machine feet for the projects in this book are:

Clear view foot A transparent foot, this enables you to see where you are going. I use this as my basic foot.

Zipper foot This type of foot, with its small footprint, allows you to sew very close to a folded edge. This is extremely useful for sewing in zips (hence the name) but also with the book stack technique on pages 98–101.

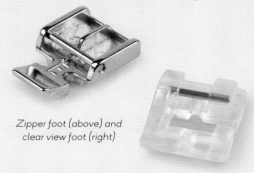

Zipper foot (above) and clear view foot (right)

Sewing machine needles

Basic sewing machine needles are commonly available in sizes 70, 80, 90, 100 and 110 (US 10, 12, 14, 16, and 18). The smaller the number, the finer the needle. A thin size 70 (US 10) needle will punch a small hole, suitable for sewing fine fabrics like cotton lawn. In contrast, a thick size 110 (US 18) needle is stout enough to punch a large hole into tough fabrics. For the work in this book the most useful sizes are 70 and 80 (US 10 and 12).

A ball point machine needle is useful when using a knitted fabric. This type of needle pushes its way through a gap in the knit rather than piercing the threads of the fabric, which helps to prevent the machine from 'choking up'.

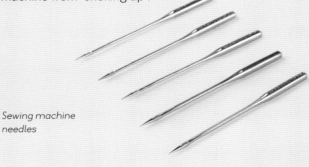

Sewing machine needles

Other materials

The following tools and equipment are important too; they will make your working much easier and more enjoyable, which will bring better results.

Rotary cutters This is a hand-held cutting wheel that makes cutting the edges of finished samples easier than with scissors.

Self-healing cutting mat Place your fabrics on this mat when cutting with a rotary cutter. The grid lines will help you to cut straight lines, and the score marks will close up to leave a smooth surface.

Rotary slashing tool Similar to a rotary cutter, this has a guide to stop you cutting through to the back of the stack. It is best used when slashing straight lines in large projects.

Pins Long glass-headed pins which do not melt under the iron are the best sort to use for general pinning.

Appliqué pins These are short and sharp, which makes them useful for awkward places where long pins might get in the way.

Sewing clips These are little clips that hold layers together. Small bulldog clips can be used but will not grip quite so well.

Fusible interfacing I avoid glue at all costs. It is a quick fix that will soon go a nasty colour and spoil your work. Instead, use an iron-on cotton interfacing like StayFlex to apply the pattern or design on the base of the fabric stack. It is translucent so designs can be traced from your own drawings. One important fact to remember when working from the back of a stack is that your designs will be reversed. Just remember to mark the designs with a permanent pen on the glue side of the interfacing.

Paper Cartridge paper can be used in place of fusible interfacing for transferring the design to small samples. Large and small sheets of paper can be used for samples, while a roll of wallpaper lining paper is very handy when designing large projects.

Pencil and eraser These are the bare essentials for design work. An HB or 2B pencil will work perfectly.

White marker or tailor's chalk These are useful for transferring designs onto dark fabrics.

Fabric markers Many of my techniques are washed at the end. There are various types of fabric markers on the market, so pick one that will wash out if you choose to use them. Personally, I prefer to use a sharp lead pencil or propelling pencil. Used very lightly, it will come off with an eraser or light wash.

Black permanent marker pen This is used for transferring patterns on to paper or fusible interfacing. The ink needs to be permanent so it will not bleed when the fabric is washed.

Masking tape Low-tack masking tape is useful for holding the patterns to the table when tracing off the design.

Rulers A variety of lengths are useful. I have a 30cm (12in) acrylic ruler and a longer metal ruler.

45° angle and set square While not essential, both of these are useful for measuring angles accurately.

A pair of compasses These make drawing perfect circles – something used for Essex puffs and other advanced techniques – a breeze.

Notebook and large sticky labels Keeping notes about each sample you make is very useful. There are many different permutations and variations that you can try for your fabric art: different colourways, different fabrics and so forth. Innovative ideas always seem to come while you are doing something else – be ready to capture them! Make a note of such ideas to help you remember to try another day, then number the labels and stick them to the back of your samples.

The bare essentials

BASIC SEWING KIT

The projects in this book all require a basic sewing kit. This is made up of the following simple materials:

- *Selection of hand sewing needles*
- *Small scissors*
- *Pins*
- *White and black sewing cotton*

All about layering

Layering is the technique of combining different colours and textures of fabric, securing them together with machine stitch and then cutting or slashing some away to reveal the layers of cloth below. The resulting textile is richly textured and can be further enhanced by washing, creating a lively and unique piece of textile art that can be used for wall hangings, interiors or clothing. This wonderful technique enables you to play with shapes and colour combinations. It is sometimes called reverse appliqué because, rather than adding fabrics onto a base as with traditional appliqué, you instead stack the fabrics first and then remove some. With practice, the colours revealed can be controlled to enhance and complement each other. Their juxtaposition can even enable colours to mix in the eye.

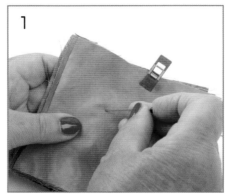

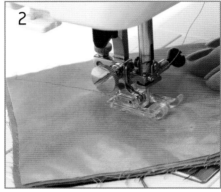

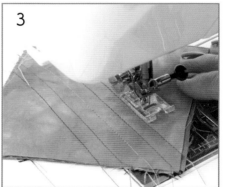

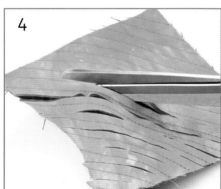

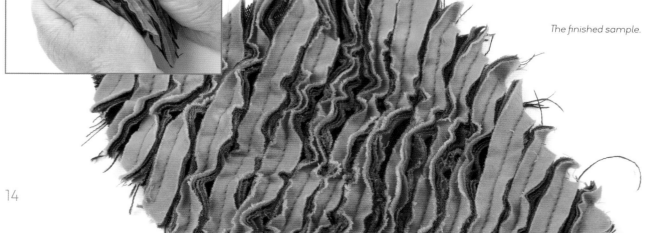

The layering technique

This is the basic technique that underlies all the other layering and slashing techniques.

1 Select six different colours of lightweight fabric. Cut six 10cm (4in) squares; one from each fabric. Stack the fabrics one on top of another, then pin or clip them together.

2 Select a machine thread which matches the top fabric and use this in the bobbin and on top of the machine. Sew a straight line across the bias of the fabric from corner to corner.

3 Using the width of the machine foot as a guide to space the lines, continue to sew parallel lines. Secure the beginning and the end of each line of sewing (use a lock stitch if your machine has one, or a few backward stitches if not).

4 Use scissors or a seam ripper to cut between the lines through all but the base layer.

5 Wash the fabric, then rub and twist the sample vigorously. Squeeze dry. Rub and tousle the fabric whilst it dries. This is called making the fabric 'bloom'.

The finished sample.

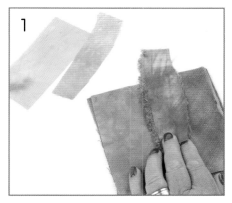

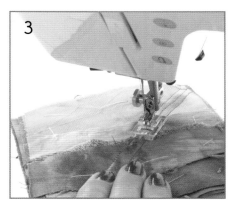

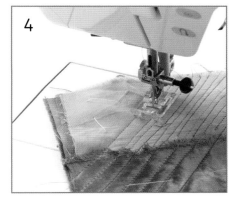

Adding a pieced layer

Rather than using a single piece of fabric on a layer, you can use a pieced layer: one made from a patchwork of strips, squares or torn pieces of different fabrics.

This method can be adapted to suit many designs. Here, I use four strips – the blue and lilac will represent the sky in a simple landscape.

1 Stack five squares of a variety of fabrics on top of a base layer of sturdy fabric. Next, arrange a sixth layer made from several strips of fabric on top.

2 Lightly tack the sixth pieced layer to the stack using a sewing needle and white thread, to create a six-layer stack.

3 Machine parallel lines from corner to corner, then add an extra line between the two, stopping where the lilac meets the green. This helps to differentiate the sky and land areas of this landscape.

4 Continue until you have machined over the whole surface (as with the layering technique opposite).

5 Cut between the lines of the top five fabrics, leaving the sturdy base layer intact.

6 Remove any tacking stitching, then wash and bloom the stack (see step 5, opposite) to finish.

TIP

You may find the seam ripper more convenient for cutting between narrow lines.

The finished sample.

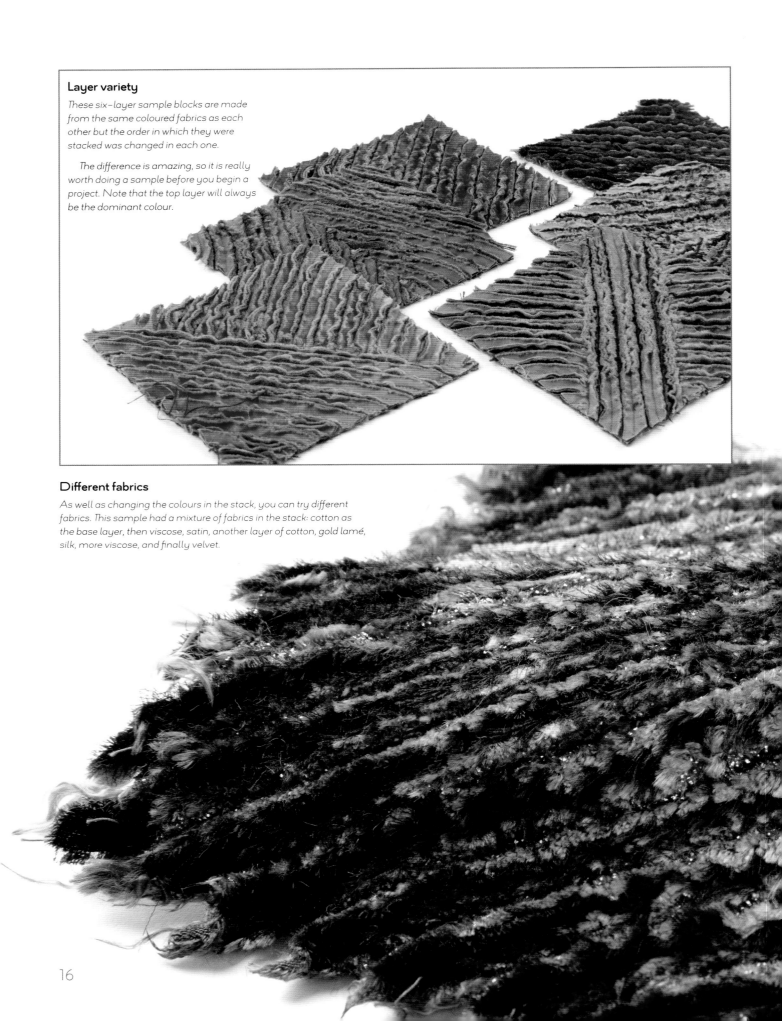

Layer variety

These six-layer sample blocks are made from the same coloured fabrics as each other but the order in which they were stacked was changed in each one.

The difference is amazing, so it is really worth doing a sample before you begin a project. Note that the top layer will always be the dominant colour.

Different fabrics

As well as changing the colours in the stack, you can try different fabrics. This sample had a mixture of fabrics in the stack: cotton as the base layer, then viscose, satin, another layer of cotton, gold lamé, silk, more viscose, and finally velvet.

Breaking the rules

The samples on pages 14–16 show the lines and slashing on the bias of the fabric. This is the best way to prevent fraying. However, breaking this rule is a lot of fun, and creates fantastic results! The following ideas will give you some alternative ideas to try when experimenting with the layering technique.

- Sewing the lines with the grain of the fabric results in a lot more fraying. Some fabrics will fray more than others. Loose-weave fabrics like silk dupion, for example, will almost fall to bits but tighter-weave cotton will give a hairy result.

- Curved lines of stitching are a very useful mark to represent water or sky in a design. They will also create an interesting effect – the fraying will only occur on part of the line, because the thread goes with the grain in some places and against the grain in others.

- Varying the width between the parallel lines will enable you to create yet another texture. It is useful if you are trying to show proportion or perspective in a scene.

Top: the sewn lines were sewn going with the grain of the fabric, resulting in lots of fraying and loose threads

Middle: Using curved lines is very useful when making a representational design.

Bottom: The width between the parallel lines was varied for this sample – a useful technique when creating perspective effects.

Tall Trees

This large piece – it measures 130 x 90cm (51 x 35½in) – demonstrates the use of cuts and slashes at various lengths. The pieces closer to the bottom get larger, which helps to create a sense of distance and perspective. The undercolours used towards the bottom are also darker to increase the visual weight of the piece in this area. The tree trunks were added on top of the slashed yellow area.

Rising Leaves

The leaf-shaped holes in this sample are held open with long straight stitches on a background of slashed lines. Note that the parallel lines change direction in some places, giving the impression of a stalk to the leaves and flowers. This also gives a bit of relief to the background.

Fringe edging and bindings

Making a fringe edge or binding strip can be a useful and delightful way to decorate plainer fabrics or edge the slashed work. The distance between the lines will determine the depth of the fringe. This can be the width of the machine foot for a small fringe or binding, up to around 5cm (2in) for a deeper fringe.

As the strips are created on the bias, it is easy to apply them to curves. Deeper strips may need to have a few snips in them before they are washed and agitated to make them integrate and bloom.

Making the fringe or binding strips

Begin by making a stack of fabric using several different colours that will complement or coordinate with the plain fabric that you wish to decorate with a fringe or edge. In this example I chose to decorate a five-layered stack.

TIP

Adding a little of the base colour – i.e. the same colour as the main fabric – to the fringe strip helps to visually integrate it into the finished piece.

1 As for the basic layering technique (see pages 14–17), cut 30cm (12in) squares from six to eight different coloured fabrics. Stack the fabrics and sew parallel diagonal lines across the square. Cut between the sewn lines, right through the whole stack. This leaves you with lots of strips (see inset).

2 Machine all the parallel lines as for the layering technique. Here I have changed the direction of the lines in each quarter to add interest.

3 Place the strips on the stack and sew them on with the sewing machine, sewing on top of the previous stitching line. The strips are cut on the bias so can easily be applied in curved patterns if required. Corners can be mitred or cut square.

4 Working layer by layer, cut into the fringe strips. This will enable them to fluff up and integrate with the base.

5 Slash between the lines of top layers of the base, leaving the bottom layer intact.

6 Wash the project with the applied strips. Agitate and rub the strips to allow them to 'fluff out' and bloom.

TIP

Tumble dry for a good effect.

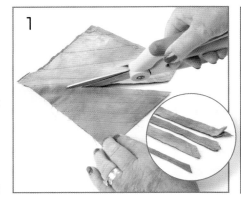

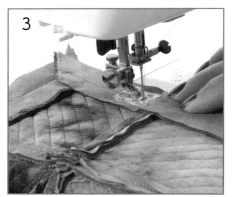

Curving fringes

The base of this sample is worked on a stack of yellows and reds. Curved parallel lines were machined through the layers, then all bar one of the parallel line spaces were slashed. The remaining intact line was left uncut and later decorated with French knots.

To the yellow base blue fringe strips were added in two different widths. These were made as shown opposite, and then applied to the yellow base. The result is impressively intricate, but it is in fact a very simple process.

Inserting a stack

When planning a project, you may find that there are small areas that need extra colours or additional layers This technique allows you to introduce specific colours or textures in just part of your project. Imagine a night sky constructed from lots of layers of blues and navy – in one corner you want to show a bright moon and you have no yellows in your stack. This is the time to insert a stack.

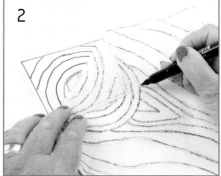

1 Draw your design on paper using a black marker pen. Mark the moon area to differentiate areas A and B.

2 Place some fusible interfacing on top of the design, with the glue side uppermost. Trace the design using a black permanent marker.

3 Place the marked interfacing on the back of the base fabric, glue side down, and iron it on.

TIP

Tracing the design onto the glue side of the interfacing ensures that the design is reversed for you; but the design can be mirrored simply by placing the design on the back of the stack.

4 Make a four-piece stack of navy, black and dark blues, the same size as the design on the base fabric.

5 Make a smaller stack of yellows and golds, large enough to cover the area of the moon. Lift the top layer of the blue stack away slightly and place the small yellow stack where the moon will appear.

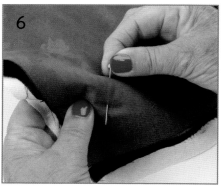

6 Replace the top blue layer. Hold both stacks in place with a few tacking stitches or pins through all the layers to ensure that everything stays in place.

7 Turn the stack over so the interfacing is uppermost. Using a blue bobbin, machine the circle marked in red.

8 Remove the fabric from the machine and cut away the top blue layer from the circle, working closely to the machined line.

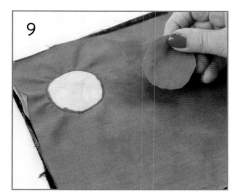

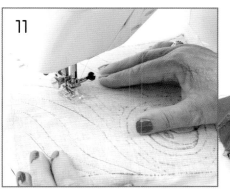

9 Cut away one layer of yellow from area A.

10 Cut away three layers of yellow from area B.

11 Machine, then slash between all the lines, leaving the base blue fabric intact.

12 Wash and thoroughly agitate and rub the finished piece. Gradually the yellow will begin to show through, giving a wonderful painterly effect.

The finished piece.

Another example of inserting a stack

In this example, a small stack of reds was placed in the centre of mixed yellow fabrics, under the top layer of yellow. This gives you control: however you slash or cut, the red will only show in the central area of the design.

Grids

Using a machined grid of squares or rectangles enables you to slash within a shape to reveal the colours and cloth beneath without risking the layers falling apart. A template is necessary for this technique. I always use two colours for my grids, so that I can easily tell the difference between the sewing lines – those you follow to secure the layers together – and the slashing lines, which you cut into.

Using a grid for layering and slashing

You can photocopy or scan this grid, attach it to the back of a stack and sew through the paper and the grid. If you choose this approach, the paper layer needs to be ripped away after sewing and before washing.

Alternatively, try tracing the grid onto the glue side of fusible interfacing using a permanent marker, then ironing it onto the back of your stack. The interfacing can remain in place on the stack.

You could also try making a grid of your own in another size. Be careful not to make the grid so small that the slashing is too difficult.

TIP

Be mindful of which colours you choose. The top colour will always dominate. The other fabric will be revealed in places where you slash through.

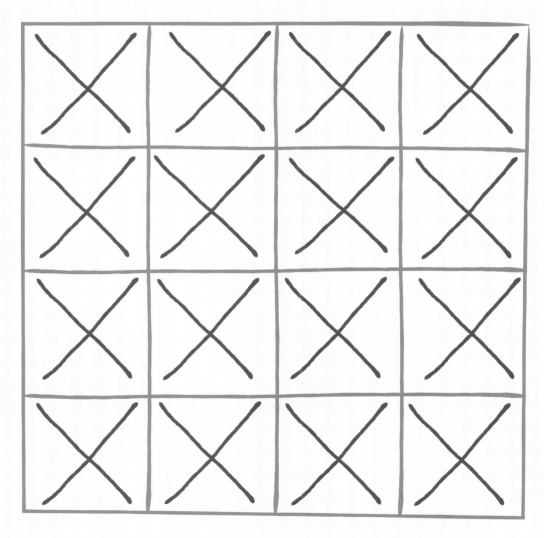

Grid template

This template is shown at actual size. The sewing lines are marked in blue and the slashing lines are marked in red.

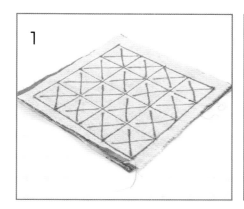

1 Trace the grid onto fusible interfacing, glue side up, using a permanent marker. You should be able to see the marking on the non-glue side. Iron it onto the back of a four-layer stack, 1cm (½in) larger than the grid.

2 Place the stack with the fusible interfacing uppermost under the sewing machine. Ensure that the bobbin thread matches the top fabric. Machine all the blue lines carefully in straight stitch.

3 From the front of the stack, begin to cut where indicated by the red slashing lines. Cut down to the colour you wish to reveal. Keep in mind which is your last colour before you reach the white interfacing. Take care not to cut into the machine line.

4 Flip open some of the cut flaps. You can secure them open with a few embroidery stitches, or just wash the piece and allow it to bloom as normal. While it remains wet, you can manipulate some of the flaps for the desired effect.

The finished piece.

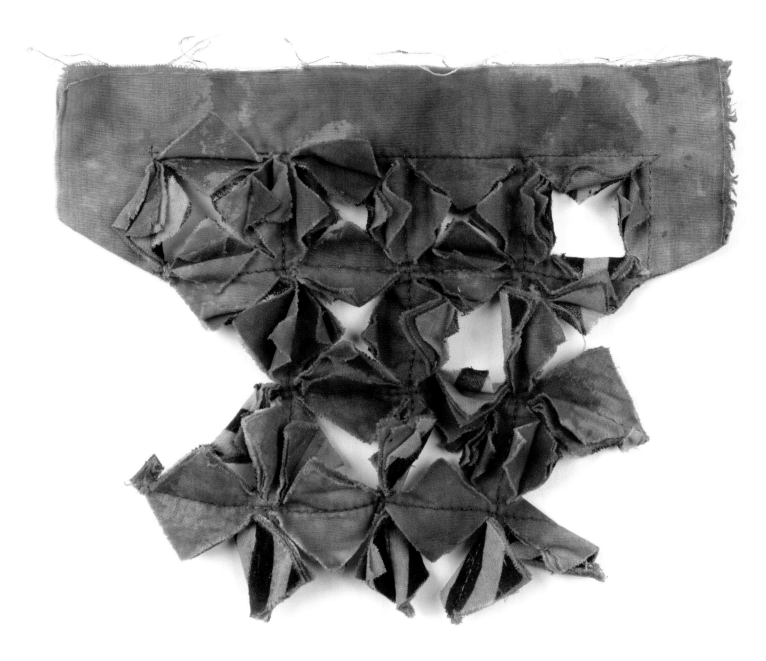

Little green grid sample

To demonstrate the flexibility and variety the grid can give you, this sample was also created using the grid template on page 24. Cotton fabric with printed stripes was selected for one of the layers, which gives great visual interest to the loose, lacy finished result.

For this very different effect, you need to draw the grid on the back of the base layer and omit the interfacing. Continue the cutting right to the edges and the excess fabric will drop away, leaving a decorative edge. The cutting has be taken through all the layers, including the backing. Scrunch and separate the layers after washing to give the full effect.

Little Christmas coloured grid sample

In this sample, which again uses the template on page 24, the grid was marked directly onto the back of the base layer and the slashing cut right through to the back – though note that care must be taken not to cut through the stitched grid. The finished piece is reversible and stretchy. The edges have also been cut through to make a decorative edge.

Grid template

*This template is shown at actual size.
The sewing lines are marked in blue and
the slashing lines are marked in red.
There is no need to machine the grid,
which is shown in green for reference.*

Grids as guides

The grid can make it easier to design other shapes. Here we look at making leaf and flower shapes.

1 Make a stack of five different fabrics at least 1cm (½in) larger than the grid. Remember that the top layer will be most dominant in colour. Place the grid on the back of the stack.

2 Iron the stack in place. Match the bobbin thread to the top colour. Place the stack in the sewing machine with the grid side uppermost, then sew around all the blue lines. Take care to secure the beginning and ends of each line and complete each petal shape with no gaps.

3 Tidy the connecting threads on the front by carefully trimming them away with a pair of scissors.

4 From the front of the pile slash through each petal to reveal which colour you would like to show. If you are using a paper grid, remove it. Wash, agitate and bloom the piece to finish.

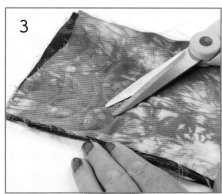

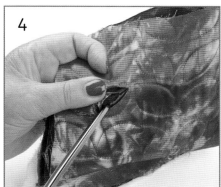

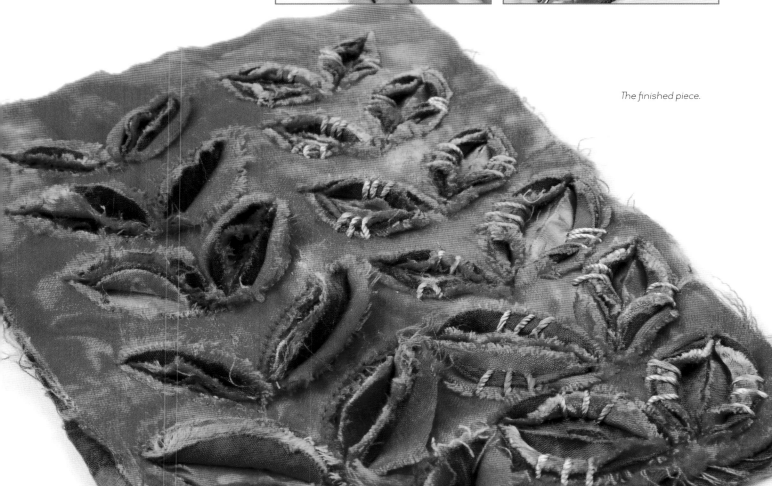

The finished piece.

Rising Red Petals

In the finished piece, some of the leaves/petals have been held open with simple stitches, while others were left unstitched to add variety. Note how the petal shapes have been made smaller as they rise to the top, simply by slitting a shorter distance along each slashing line. You may choose to play with this design, perhaps changing the direction and size of the petals.

Scattered Petals

The grid template on page 28 was used for this example, although alternate rows of the petal/leaf shapes have been inverted. This simple change results in flower shapes radiating from central points. Where there are insufficient shapes to make a full flower, I modified the cutting to suggest leaves, which I decorated with running stitch .

The top green layer of this stack comprises green patches arranged in a considered fashion to add a great painterly effect to the surface. They were secured together with large tacking stitches, rather than in a traditional patchwork style, in order to keep the design loose. Any flapping pieces of green cloth can be secured with some simple mark-making straight stitches if necessary.

Mixing grids and lines

It is important to note that using a grid will result in your design being mirrored in the final piece, because the working is done from the back. This asymmetrical example is a demonstration of the principle.

   If it is essential that your design is not mirrored, be sure to mark the design on the glue side of the interfacing. This will flip the design for you.

Grid template

This template is shown at actual size. The sewing lines are marked in blue and the slashing lines are marked in red. The green lines are shown for reference only.

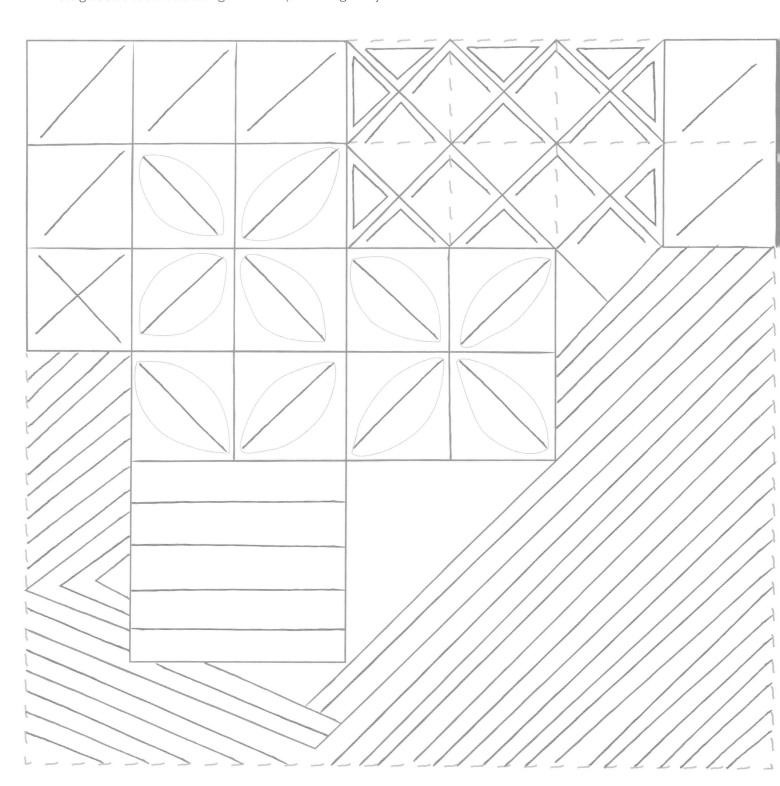

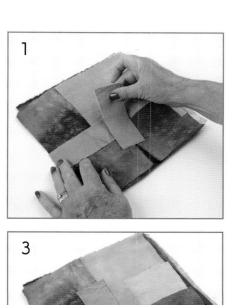

1 Make a stack of three layers, a little bigger than the grid pattern to allow for a border, then add a fourth pieced layer (see page 15) from patches of harmonious colours (i.e. those close to each other on the colour wheel). Do not pin or tack the layers.

2 Prepare a multi-coloured stack of five layers that is roughly the size and shape of the triangle marked with parallel lines at the top right of the grid template (see inset). Gently lift the corner of the patched layer and insert the triangular stack.

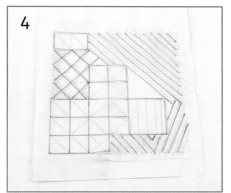

3 Replace the top layer and carefully tack the whole sample with large stitches.

4 Cut a piece of woven fusible interfacing a little bigger than the grid. Lay it glue side up on the grid and stick the edges down with a few pieces of masking tape to hold it still. Trace the blue grid onto the interfacing with a permanent marker pen.

TIP

It is important to mark the glue side as this grid is asymmetrical and will be reversed for you with this technique.

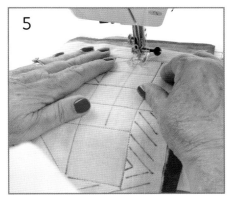

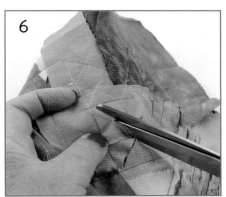

5 Iron the interfacing onto the back of the stack of fabrics, then place a bobbin in your machine with thread to match the pieced layer. Place the stack under the sewing machine with the interfacing uppermost and sew the blue lines of the grid.

6 Remove the tacking, then begin slashing where indicated in red on the grid. Do not slash lower than the last colour (i.e. the bottommost fabric in the stack).

7 Where the red lines extend over the green dotted lines, cut right over the edge to create a fringe.

8 Wash, agitate and bloom the sample.

The finished piece

The combination of grids and lines makes this piece appear far more complex than the earlier samples, but the underlying principles are just the same as those simpler versions. Here, the top layer is constructed of pieces of blue, purple and pink. A stack of various colours has been placed under the parallel lines as this parallel line slashing looks better with more layers and adds some extra contrast.

As I have not trimmed the edge of this sample at the edge of the parallel lines, it has left a wonderful fringe effect. This is something to bear in mind for another project.

Compare the finished piece to the grid template on page 32 to note how the design is mirrored by the process.

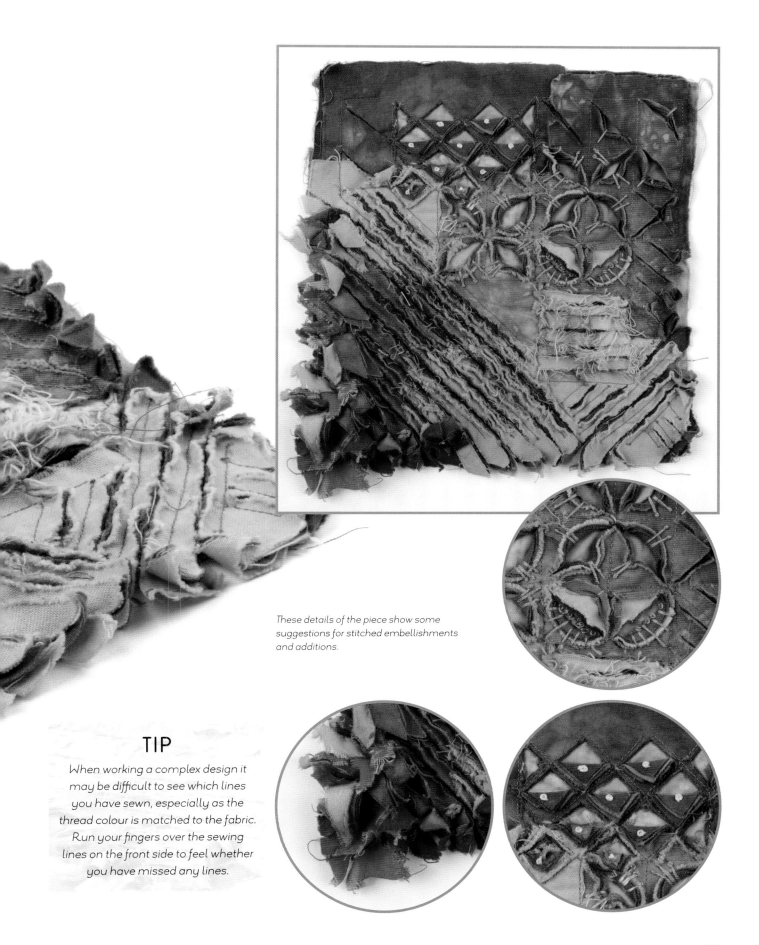

These details of the piece show some suggestions for stitched embellishments and additions.

TIP

When working a complex design it may be difficult to see which lines you have sewn, especially as the thread colour is matched to the fabric. Run your fingers over the sewing lines on the front side to feel whether you have missed any lines.

Hand stitch embellishment

The fabric manipulation techniques earlier alter the surface of the cloth and leave little pockets that beg to be filled in with a few simple stitches. Hand embroidery can be used to enhance the appearance, add small details, and also to hold some of the layers open.

Straight stitch

Sometimes referred to as flat stitch, straight stitch is a simple sewing stitch in which individual stitches are made without crossing or looping the thread, as shown in the diagram here. These versatile stitches are generally used to form a broken or unbroken line, and can also make starbursts, create geometric designs and fill shapes, as shown in the example below.

Straight stitch

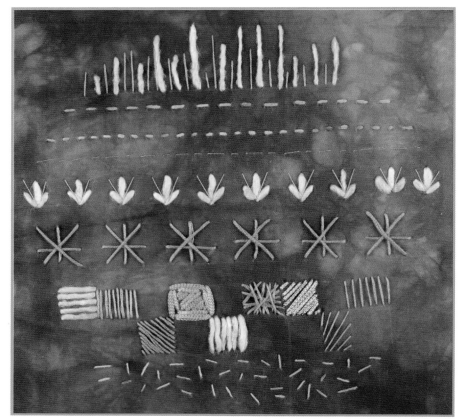

Opposite:

Red Hot Lupin

Simple straight stitches have been used to decorate the layered cloth. Some long, some short, some shiny and some dull. The stitches not only enhance the piece but also hold open some of the layers.

Geometric lines

Endless shapes are possible with lines of straight stitch. To add interest, vary the colour and thickness of the threads.

In and out in a line

As this stitch can be very subtle you might choose to use a thick thread. If you do so, I suggest that you mark the fabric and follow the line.

Motifs

Individual straight stitches can be arranged in a starburst or spray shape.

Scatter–fill

Fill a shape with straight stitches close together or scatter the stitches randomly or in a more organised fashion.

Chain stitch petals

Detached chain stitch

38

Chain stitch

A chain stitch is a looped stitch which can be used along a curved or straight line. Chain stitch results in bold marks resembling a chain or rope, which gives the stitch its name.

It can also be used as an individual stitch and is then called a detached chain. A detached chain stitch can represent a flower petal or even a rain drop.

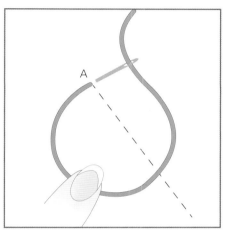

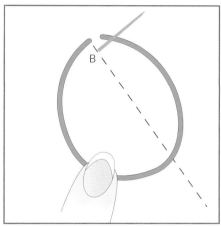

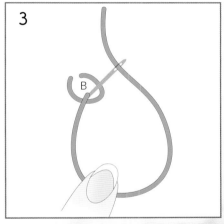

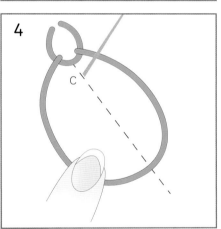

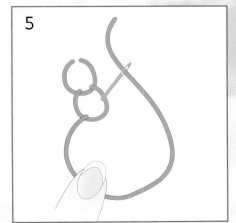

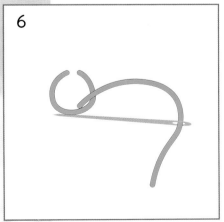

1 Bring the thread through at A, then hold the thread down with your thumb. Insert the needle through the same hole at A.

2 Bring the needle out at B, within the loop.

3 Keeping the thread under the needle point, pull the loop of thread to form a chain. Hold the thread down with the thumb and insert the needle down through the same hole at B.

4 Bring the needle out at C.

5 Hold the thread down with the thumb and insert the needle down through the same hole at C. Continue working stitches in the same way.

6 To finish the chain, use a small tying stitch to secure the final loop. One stitch on its own like the last stitch is called a detached chain stitch.

French knots

As the name suggests, this stitch creates decorative little knots. If the thread is not pulled through evenly, it will leave a loop instead of a knot. These loops, which I like to call lazy knot loops, can be attractive in their own right, so do not worry if your first attempts at French knots leave you with loops. They are delightful when used in clusters or individually as little 'bullet marks'.

You can also create French knots with stems on, which are both functional and decorative, appearing like the stamens of a flower.

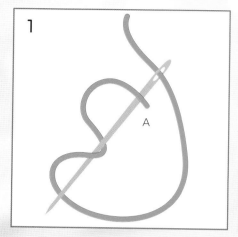 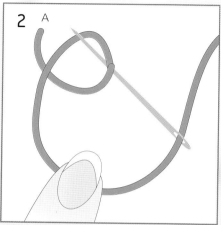 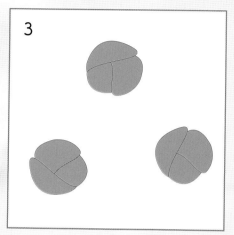

1 You will need to use a fairly thick thread as a thin knot will be rather insignificant when used on the layered fabric. Bring the needle through from the back of the fabric at A, the place where the knot is to be positioned. Encircle the thread twice with the needle.

2 Holding the thread firmly with the thumb, twist the needle back to A and insert it close to where the thread first emerged.

3 Holding the knot down with the thumb, pull the thread through at the back and secure it with a small stitch.

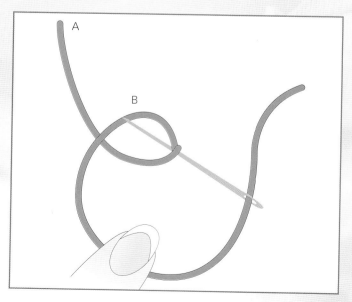

French knots with stems

Bring the needle out where you want the stem to begin (A). Holding the thread firmly with the thumb, twist the needle into the place where you wish to position the knot at B.

Open triangle windows

This piece uses long-stemmed French knots to decorate and hold open some slashed areas on layered fabrics.

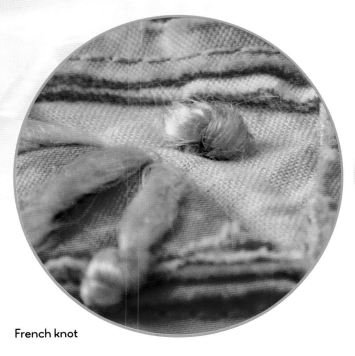

French knot

French knot with a stem

Kantha

Kantha is a type of embroidery from eastern South Asia, most often associated with Bangladesh. Old saris are traditionally stacked on top of each other and hand-stitched to make a thin, textured piece of cushion, light blanket, throw or bedspread. I use it in my work to control layers of unstitched fabric and to create a rippled effect on the surface.

Linear style

This approach creates the impression of attractive ripples in the work, that can lead the viewer's eye. You can keep them straight, or incorporate long curves; just keep the rows close to each other.

1 Select an area of your layered work that has not been cut away.

2 Choose a thread to match the top fabric so as to blend in and to leave the lovely texture to speak for itself. I choose to use three strands of soft cotton embroidery thread.

3 Beginning from the top right-hand corner, with a knot placed on the underside. Work running stitches along the cloth toward the left side, taking up small areas of the cloth at intervals. I like the stitches to be a little smaller than the spaces between each stitch. Slightly tug the thread to increase the puckering effect.

4 Begin a new row parallel to the previous one. The space between the rows should be the same as the gap between each stitch.

5 The stitches on each new row should fall slightly behind the stitches in the preceding or succeeding rows. This manner of working produces the rippled effect.

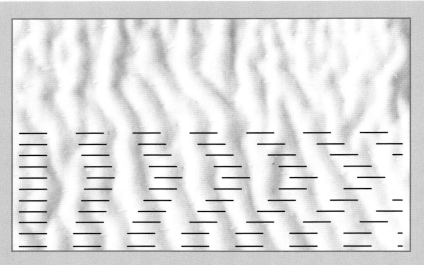

The dotted lines overlaid on the lower half indicate rows of running stitch.

TIP

These are the rules but feel free to break them for your own unique effect. A few ideas: change the scale; work on sheer fabric; or use a really thick thread.
A wonderfully sumptuous effect is achieved when kantha stitch is worked on velvet.

Spiral style

Small children seem to like to playing with the little lumps this spiralling method creates – I have seen one or two suck them as a comforter!

1 Lightly pencil the spiral design onto the layered fabric if you prefer some guidelines.

2 Begin at the centre of the spiral and work the stitches in the same way as the linear style (see above), working around the spiral.

3 Gently tugging the central stitches of the spiral will cause a little bump to appear. If you do not like this bump, then do not pull quite as tightly.

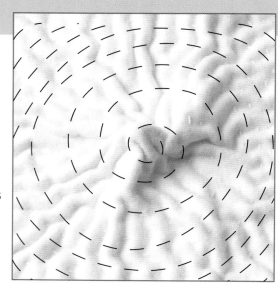

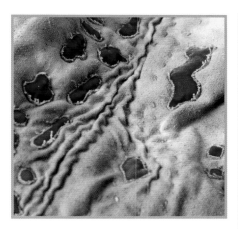

Fish kimono

While experimenting with ways to create the fish skin effect, I found that velvet shifted all over the place once covered with silk noil – not an ideal combination! After cutting shapes away to reveal the red velvet beneath I was left with a lot of baggy silk noil which needed to be controlled. Stabbing into it with kantha stitch did the trick and enhanced the surface at the same time.

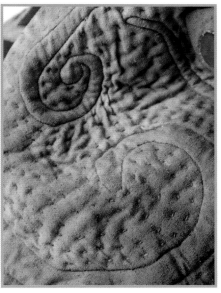

Kantha for contol

This area was quite lumpy and the kantha stitches helped to control and flatten the fabric.

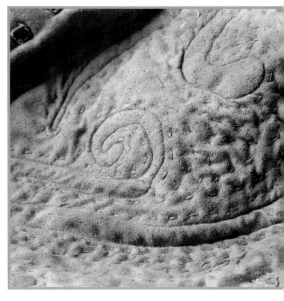

Water effects

The tiny kantha stitches made the fabric ripple in a very water–like fashion.

INSPIRATION & DESIGN

Sea shells

The design for this piece was inspired by a collection of sea shells on the beach. Once transferred to a stack of muted coloured fabrics, and after the machining and slashing, wire wool was placed on and allowed to rust to produce the rich, naturalistic oranges.

Finding ideas

'Just show up and get to work. The best ideas come out of the
process: they come out of the work itself.'

Thomas 'Chuck' Close (b. 1940)

In my experience, inspiration never comes when sitting looking at
a blank page, so get yourself out and about. Look, see, record and
absorb all you can. The design process can be learned but there is
no substitute for filling your brain with new experiences, smells,
sights and sounds. You need to put something in your head to get
something out.

Initial inspiration

Much of my inspiration comes from my
surroundings in the countryside. It also seems
to suit my technique. It gives me a view from a
distance and also plenty of textures to inspire
the slashing. The very best way to record this
is to paint which makes you really look. Don't
worry if you are not a master painter, just go
for it. A few photographs to go alongside it will
help too.

Be active

While I work on samples, a project or just when
having a play with fabrics and paints, I keep
my sketchbook close at hand and write a
'must-try' list.

Understanding your materials is also a great
help. After a while you can look at things and
see in your mind's eye how they could translate
into fabrics, layers and slashes.

Moodboards

Moodboard for *Rapefield on a Stormy Day*

A moodboard is a way of collecting all your ideas and viewing them all in one place. The board itself can be anything: the side of an old cardboard box, or an old large canvas print from a charity shop is just as suitable as a purpose-made felt- or cork-covered pinboard.

Start by gathering photographs and magazine cuttings of your subject. Make a few sketches – even scribbles or doodles on the back of an envelope will do. Next, look through any previous samples and scraps of fabric, and put them with the photographs and sketches. Place anything that relates in any way to your inspiration – even small objects like old shells, bits of string or rusty nails – to one side. These will give you valuable colour and shape reference for your piece.

The next stage is to find a few mystery items: things that are not obviously related to your chosen subject but that you have a gut feeling about, such as a broken piece of sparkling jewellery, an old photograph, a piece of broken china, or a page torn from a book. These are what will make your work unique. With all these pieces to hand, you can begin to attach the items on the board. Aim to cover the board completely, and allow things to overlap: leaving patches of cork board showing adds nothing to the process. Arrange and rearrange, add more over the next few days until you get a board that reflects the mood that you are aiming for. Finally, take a photograph of the moodboard. It helps to look at it from a distance and is also a good record if you decide to change it at a later date.

Using a sketchbook to develop your ideas

Try to draw a little every day. It is a good habit that is fun to look back on. More than that, making pictures – however simple – in your sketchbook is a very useful exercise: because you spend time looking closely at what you are drawing, you start to really see the details and familiarise yourself with the subject. These little scribbles are thus more than just taking a photograph.

My first stage in working a sketchbook is to look and record. There is no right or wrong way to add your ideas and observations to the book. The only rule is get your ideas down.

I like to use a small notebook with squared paper pages – its size and round corners mean it fits neatly in my bag, and the squares suit my techniques, particularly for those based on a grid. Working on squared paper makes it easy to enlarge any designs at a later date. I just draw it again on larger squares to suit my finished work.

I only occasionally use colour at this stage; more often making notes of what colours would work. For me, I find the sketchbook more useful as a record of line and texture, light and shade. I tend to make colour sketches later, in a separate larger sketchbook, with plain paper. This allows me to play with some of the drawings from my small notebook, in colour and even cutting slashing through one page to show the page beneath.

One temptation to avoid is to being too precious with your sketchbook – using it to make a pretty book to show your friends, rather than as an immediate record of relatively unrefined sketches. I am not precious about what goes into the book and it often includes my shopping list, to-do lists and holiday diary. By using it both for my art and for more everyday events, I ensure that using it becomes a habit. Remember that the sketchbook is, first and foremost, yours. It is a personal tool.

A sample of my sketchbooks and colour sketches.

You can do more with sketchbooks than simply draw in them. Here I have cut and folded pages to create an interesting effect and experiment with layers on the squared paper..

EAGLES CLAW

Interpreting your inspiration into fabric

Although small details can be added with stitch at the end of making your fabric artwork, my layering technique requires a robust design with not too many fiddly details. As you become more familiar with the technique, you will begin to notice that there are some shapes that work better than others, and also what scale suits best.

Many crafts benefit from the source image being abstracted slightly as this makes the interpretation of the image more striking and more effective. Layering is no exception. There are a number of ways to approach abstracting your sketches, which will depend on what it is you are inspired by. On these pages I explain some approaches and examples of abstracting your work to make it work better with the layering technique.

Abstracting and stylising – creating a working sketch

Squinting at your image will help to remove fine detail; reducing the image to bolder, stronger shapes. This makes it easier to simplify it. Look for strong horizontal, vertical or diagonal lines as the basis, then add stylised versions of large or dominant features such as buildings, trees, flowers or figures. A house might be represented as a square block, for example, while a tree can be a simple lollipop shape. Don't be tempted to overdraw the image by adding too much detail.

Take a good look at your stylised drawing and consider whether it needs further simplification. This means altering the shape of some of the features to suit your work, or even eliminate some of them altogether. For example, if you have drawn a curved path in a landscape, consider whether it might work better with a straight path. A complex, wiggly-edged pond may look better as a cleaner oval. Finally, add some textural marks – these will be used to suggest the shapes and movement in the image. Try to use the marks you have seen used in the grid cuttings earlier (see pages 24–35).

The examples on these pages show how I went about stylising, simplifying and adding texture to a few different images to produce working sketches. Practise using some of your own sketches.

Landscape

In the landscape here, you can see strong horizontal lines where the colour and texture change. Horizontal strips of colour work well with landscapes, so look for these when selecting an image.

With the horizontal lines marked on the paper, I began to look for other large features. In this case they were trees, and I marked them on the drawing in a very simple fashion. Now I added some textural marks – simple straight lines – to denote grasses. To decide on the direction for the grasses, I looked at the direction of the grasses on the source image (see left). Where they were upright, I drew them as near-vertical. Where they were bent in the wind, I used more angled lines.

Fish

The skin of this fish was of more interest than the shape of the whole fish so a small section was taken and abstracted. The dominant features of the detail are the eye, a section of the fin, and the patterns of lines and dots on the skin.

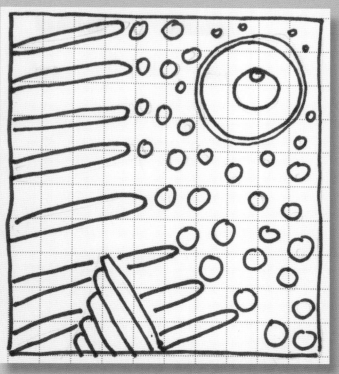

TIP

Be quick! Allow yourself only a few minutes to draw your simple image. One or two minutes is ample.
You might also try drawing your image upside down. Both of these tricks help you to record only the basic information.

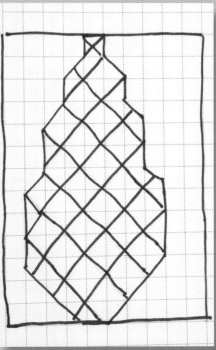

Lupin

At first glance, some objects can appear quite complex, but breaking them down reveals them to be much simpler than they first appear. This lupin is a good example. The initial impression is complex, but closer examination reveals it to be simply a cluster of blooms on a tapering stem. The blooms gradually become smaller towards the top.

The next stage is to change the blooms to a shape that works with my technique: diamonds or small squares. The result is the simple shape shown on the right. This may look a little abstract, but when the colour is added back with the fabric it will become more lupin-like again.

From sketch to working design

The process of developing our sketch will have given us lots of ideas, marks and images. These need to be made to work together in order to create a full working design and a pattern to work from.

The marks made on the working sketch (see page 50) need to be translated into marks that will work with the layering and slashing technique. The finished full working design can be traced and transferred to paper or interfacing ready to begin.

The working sketch

This simple abstracted drawing inspired by the rapeseed fields on the mood board on page 47.

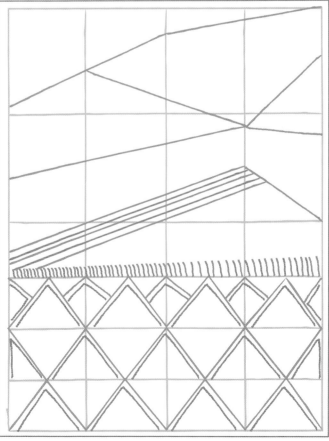

Translating the design into a grid

The design has to be further developed in order to work with the layering technique. For example, the curved lines in the sky area have been altered to become more angular, creating a sky made up of blocks – these can inform the placement of fabric and slashes. It is not necessary to draw in every single line. In this example, I have only drawn lines to indicate where I want to change the direction of the larger sections of fabric.

My first drawing shows the rapeseed as circles which are larger at the bottom, getting smaller towards the top. As this technique does not work well with small circles, I have chosen to use diamond shapes to recreate the impression of the rape blooms.

This stage requires you to make decisions. The sky area could have remained as in the working sketch, with curving lines, but I chose to use shifting planes of straight lines to emphasise the active, slightly threatening nature of the leaden sky. The bottom section of the design is very busy and I wanted to create a good contrast between the yellow rapeseed and the sky – so the areas in the sky need to be relatively large and more irregular.

The working design

The green lines indicate the grid, the blue lines are the sewing lines and the red lines show you where to cut.

Detail from the finished piece

This relatively simple landscape of a blue—grey sky over a field of yellow blooms became a joy to work on after I had drawn, looked and played with the design many times. I began to realise how menacing the sky, with its approaching rain clouds, could appear; I had the chance to try out different marks to translate this.

The sharp yellow of the blooms was, on closer inspection, revealed to be made up of countless tiny units of orange, reds and greens alongside the yellow. This informed me as to which colours needed to rise from beneath the assortments of yellows and ochres.

The full piece can be seen on pages 2–3.

Adapting a working design – converting to a grid

Your sketch may not naturally align to a grid – this is often the case with single objects or organic shapes. In these cases, you can start by using a pencil and ruler to draw a grid over your working sketch, then ensuring the elements you want to include – in this example, the flower shapes– align to the grid. This may mean enlarging individual petals to fit them more fully within a grid square, or reducing them so that a whole flower (or other relevant design element) can fit into one square.

The working sketch

A very simple abstracted drawing of flowers in a field. The centres of the flowers have been left out, but could be embroidered on at the end of the final piece. The vertical lines represent the grasses bent in the wind.

Changes to make a workable grid

The green lines here show the full grid for this working design. You will notice that the grid is broken down into smaller squares in the centre to accommodate some smaller flowers. The smaller squares in the centre have parallel lines that are designed to go with the grain of the fabric. These areas will need to be agitated particularly well in order to encourage the fabric to fray in a downward direction.

Scaling up for larger work

One of the strengths of working on a grid is that it is an easy process to convert your design to a larger size, simply by copying it onto a grid of larger squares on another piece of paper. This allows you the flexibility to work at any size. I often convert the grid so that each square measures 2.5cm (1in).

Using this approach, you can easily tell what size the finished piece will be. For example, if your design measures ten by thirty squares, you know that your finished piece will be 25 x 75cm (10 x 30in). This can be very useful when making a piece site specific (typically where a very large textile piece is required). However, there is no reason you have to stick to this size. By changing your conversion so one square equals 12.5cm (5in), the same ten by thirty square design will produce a finished piece measuring 125 x 375cm (50 x 150in).

It is a great comfort to be sure that when you have completed all the sewing and slashing, your wonderful new textile piece will be the correct size; though I would add here that you may like to allow a little for shrinkage.

TIP

Note that even if your sketch is not worked on squared paper, you can easily draw a grid over it using a pencil and ruler.

This sketchbook uses small 15mm (¹/₂in) squares, but the size of the squares in the original grid is ultimately unimportant – it is the size of the squares in your final piece that will matter.

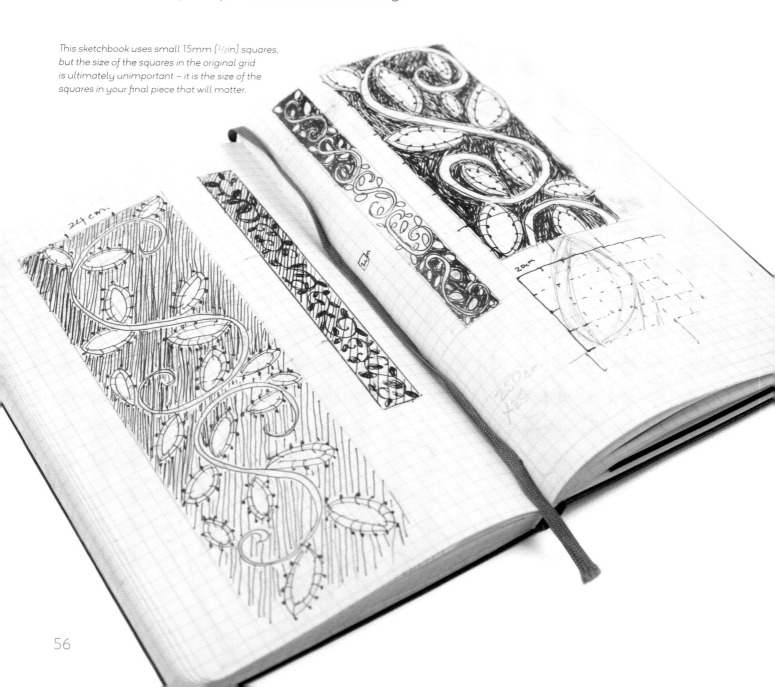

1 Draw out your planning design on squared paper using a pencil.

2 Draw a new larger grid with the same number of squares. Number the lines and rows in both grids. Working square by square, copy the design marks from the smaller grid to the larger corresponding square into the larger grid. It is best to do this with pencil so that you can adjust some of the lines if they don't feel right.

TIP

Your first attempts may give a bit of an angular result on curved areas – feel free to redraw and smooth out these lines.

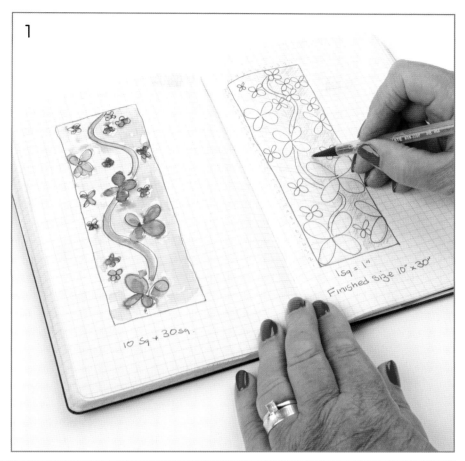

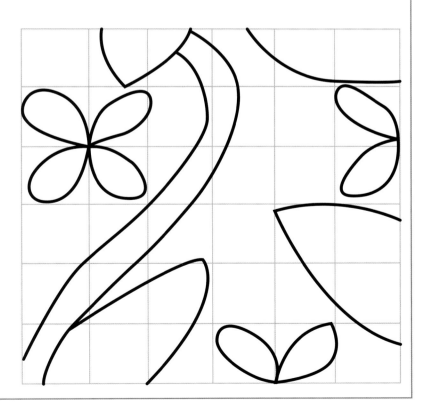

This picture shows a detail of the original sketch (left) next to an enlarged version of the same detail. Note that while the size of the individual squares is different from one detail to the other, the number of squares remains the same.

Numbering the squares makes it easier to work out where a particular line travels – it can sometimes be quite difficult to follow them, particularly when converting from very small to very large squares, or when enlarging an abstract design.

Larger pieces

For very large pieces, you may find sheets of cartridge paper are not big enough to fit your design. In these cases, I suggest using heavyweight wallpaper lining paper, which is relatively cheap, durable, and – more importantly – large enough to accommodate almost anything!

Use masking tape to stick the paper to your table, then draw on the grid with pencil. You can then proceed to transfer and scale up your design into a full working design. When you see it at full size, take a moment to refine it: you may find seeing it at the final size suggests that you add or take away some details.

Once you are happy with the pencil drawing, work over it using a permanent marker. The drawing needs to be bold as you will need to see it through the interfacing when you trace it. Do not forget to mark the outside line of the design and the margin line. You may not choose to actually sew these lines but you will need them as a guide.

Transferring the design from my sketchbook to lining paper.

The finished piece
From the 5 x 15cm (2 x 6in) sketch seen below left to the finished piece measuring 25 x 75cm (10 x 30in). Taking the design through into fabric adds depth of colour and glorious textures.

Sampling

Before plunging headlong into a new piece of work, it is advisable to try to make a small sample in order to check that your fabrics, techniques and design will all work together. This is especially useful for selecting the right fabric for your desired effect. Perhaps more importantly, it is also an opportunity to make sure that what you have designed on paper will actually work in fabric. Sometimes a design may include too much detail, which makes it difficult to sew. Sampling gives you a chance to address these issues before they become a problem, and before you have invested too much time and energy in a piece.

The best area of your design to sample is a point where there is a marked change in texture or colour, as this allows you to see the effect of different slashing marks or colours meeting will have on the layered fabric you will use. In this piece, for example, taking a sample from the sky area alone would not help you to foresee any problems that may occur in the bottom yellow area, whereas taking a section from the horizon (as shown) will highlight the challenges of both land and sky.

While you can take the detail from your initial small design, it is best to take it from the full working design as this ensures you will be working to the exact size of the proposed piece. In turn, this gives you an accurate feel for how the fabric will behave. You may find that now the design is at full size it looks a bit plain and you may need to add a few more slashing marks or add another colour in the stack or even insert a stack. You may find that a particular area in the design is too difficult to cut into and needs to be modified.

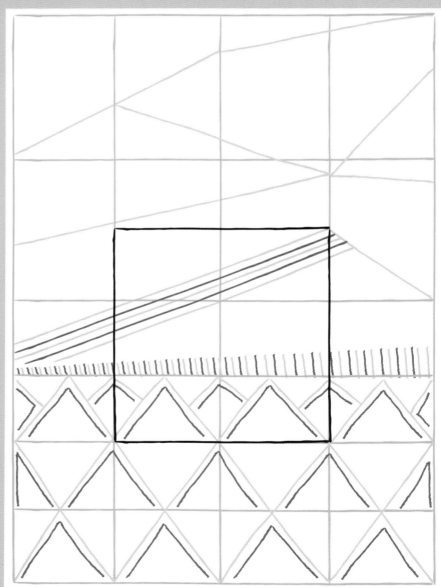

Sample selection

A small section of the design from pages 52–53 has been marked out for sampling (highlighted by the black box). Note that the area contains a variety of changes in pattern, different shapes and angles. This makes it a good representative part of the overall piece.

60

The complete sample

Based entirely on the small black-outlined section on the design opposite, this sample is an opportunity to experiment with some of the important elements of the design – the diagonal stripes and the differently sized layered triangles.

What next?

Once you have completed the sample, take a critical look at it, and decide whether you were happy with the process and results. The following questions may help you decide:

- Did the cutting reveal the colour that you wanted?
- Are any parts of the design too small to cut comfortably?
- Did the stack of fabric bloom well?

If you are not happy, then make another sample – or experiment with three or four – until all your problem areas are solved.

The following lists some approaches you might consider to help solve problems or make things easier to work:

- Consider altering the order of the stack.
- Include different fabrics or eliminate a particular fabric.
- Add more layers.
- Insert a small stack.
- Modify the design.

It is well worth going through this procedure before beginning a large piece of textile art, as it helps to prevent potential frustration and wasted time, instead making the process fun and pleasurable. I have grown to love this part of the process.

Finishing and care of your piece

Finishing your textile art piece well is important. Because the textured fabric will have been cut in various different directions, it is not always happy to hang straight. A good backing will rectify this and also give your piece a nice professional finish. Make sure that the art piece has been washed to improve the bloom and to shrink the fabric before any backing is applied.

Backing and hanging

With all those layers, the finished piece is likely to be heavy, so you will need to use a medium or heavyweight calico for the backing to provide sufficient support if you wish to display it.

To make a permanent support, you will need some 5cm (2in) wide strips of hook-and-loop fastener and a flat wooden baton approximately 2cm (¾in) smaller than the width of your finished art piece. This baton can then be used to attach the piece to the wall where it is to hang. The two hook-and-loop fastener strips will hold the work while leaving it easy to take it down to give it an occasional shake to remove any dust.

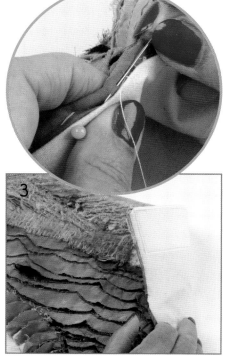

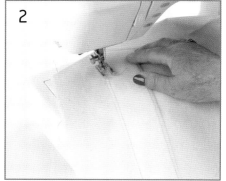

1 Cut a piece of calico large enough to allow for a good border to turn in. The backing should not show at the front at all. Fold the edges in to fit and iron it well.

2 Unfold the piece and sew on a strip of hook-and-loop fastener across the very top. This is the best time to sign the bottom of the calico or free machine your signature.

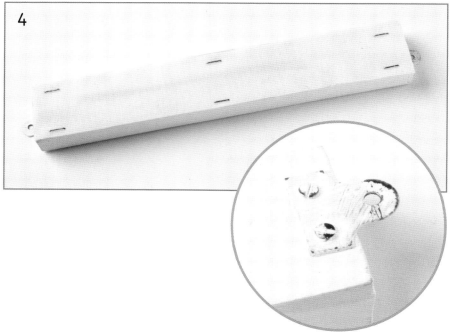

3 Fold the edges back in, then pin the backing on and stitch it to the work with a ladder stitch (see inset). Be sure to make the stitches very secure and neat.

4 Staple a matching length of hook-and-loop fastener to the flat wooden baton, then screw on mirror plates towards the ends (see inset).

Patching and repairing

Don't despair if you accidently cut through to the base layer. I do not think I have managed to make a single piece when I have not poked the scissors or the seam ripper through to the back. It is annoying but a very easy job to repair.

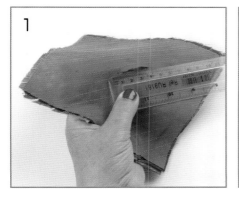

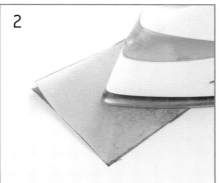

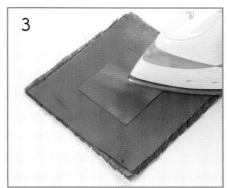

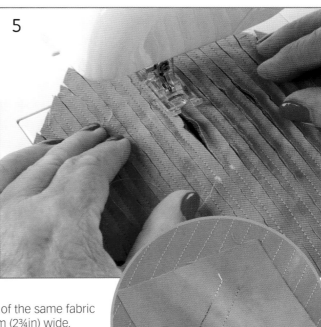

1 Measure the length of the hole you have made. Cut a rectangle of the same fabric you used as a base 4cm (1½in) longer than the hole and about 7cm (2¾in) wide.

2 Cut a piece of fusible webbing the same size as the patch. Iron the webbing onto the wrong side of the patch.

3 Allow to cool, then peel off the paper and place the patch over the hole on the backing fabric. Ensure that the patch completely covers the hole. Iron on to fuse to the backing.

4 Turn your project over with the slashed side uppermost. Use a chalk marker to make four temporary marks around the hole to show where the reinforcing stitches should go.

5 Re-machine the lines around the hole, working from dot to dot along each line of stitches that surround the hole in order to reinforce the fabric. Ensure that you match the thread with the previous sewing lines.

The repair from the back.

Textile art

The following pages walk you through the process of turning inspirational pictures into works of textile art using the techniques explained on the previous pages.

Sunset over the Sea

Whether you are using a photograph, a magazine cutting or your own artwork, it is important to select a scene that both interests and shows enough detail. While difficult details can be adjusted within the design process by stylising and modifying, you need the information there in the first place. After that, it is a case of deciding which details are of critical importance to the look you wish to achieve in your finished piece.

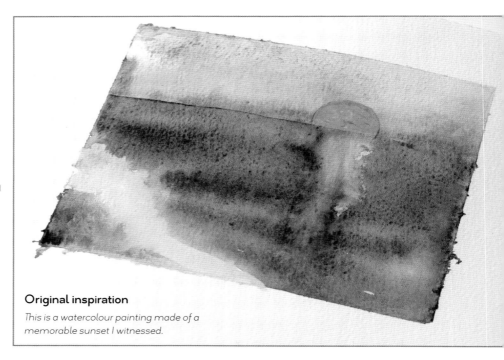

Original inspiration

This is a watercolour painting made of a memorable sunset I witnessed.

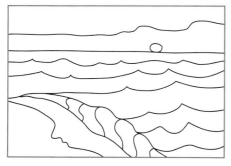

Initial design

This is a very easy picture to start with as it has simple lines. It will require a careful selection of colours.

Working design

I scaled the initial design up to full size, then prepared a detail – marked out in the box – for sampling. Note the inclusion of a grid in the detail.

Creating a sample

As described on pages 60–61, sampling a small area will help you to choose the right fabrics and to test if the slashing marks are having the effect you want. You may need to make several attempts before you come up with the most pleasing fabrics and marks.

In this example, the sample covers an area of waves, a rolling breaker and a white area of foam. The textures of these are very different, and so I spent some time selecting different fabrics and marks. The foam, for example, needed to appear clean and uniform, so there are no slashes or cuts made in it.

In contrast, the waves and breaker need to be made distinct. Since the colours needed to be shared – it's the same body of water, after all – the difference comes through using contrasting directional slashes.

Sample taken from the detail opposite

Preparing the stack

Using the original drawing and the full working design drawing as a visual reference, you can lay out the stack. This is perhaps the most important stage. Once the stack is laid out, you can machine the piece and begin cutting.

1 Gather a collection of fabrics in white, blues, greens and yellows. The more variations of each colour you can find, the richer the final effect will be. I suggest four or five different yellows, for example, along with lots of different blues and greens for the sea.

2 Lay down the interfacing with the design drawn on it, then lay a sturdy blue fabric to cover the whole design. This is the base fabric.

3 Loosely recreate the scene on top, using a strip of blue fabric for the sky, a band of yellow for the sunset, and a wider band of blue or blue-green for the sea, slightly overlapping each coloured band with the previous band. Add a band of white for foam and a darker blue across the bottom.

4 Repeat step 3 at least four more times so that your stack is five or six layers deep. Vary the specific colours of the fabrics if possible – you might use a more orange-yellow for one layer of the sunset band, for example.

5 Iron the stack to attach the interfacing, then tack through all the layers.

6 Turn the piece over so the design is uppermost, then machine the lines that edge the blocks of colour. Use a blue thread in the bobbin.

7 Cut away any fabric you wish not to show on the top surface – any blue in the sun area or blue in the white area, for example – then proceed to machine all the remaining lines.

8 Study the picture on page 67 to see where to cut. The large waves are cut just above the machined line, for example.

This detail shows how overlapping the bands of colour at the stacking stage results in a smooth blend: the sky fabrics 'bleed' nicely through and into the sunset reflections.

Allowing the sky area to overlap the orange sunset reflection allows the oranges to bleed into the sky effectively. The sun circle was machined with the rest of the stack, but the top orange layer was later removed to reveal the lighter layer beneath. Alternatively, it could have been applied at the end over the top of the slashed area, which would have given a sharper result.

These two details show different parts of the sea. The curved waves fray. A good mixture of blues, turquoise and navy in the stack has given the sea real depth. Note that the sea changes colour on the horizon – little observations like this all add up to a more realistic scene.

The finished piece

Lavender Field

I was initially attracted to this image because of the display of perspective which works well with my technique.

I made a painting of the scene, and later decided to develop it into a textile art piece. This required me to look more closely in order to understand it more and appreciate its qualities.

Original inspiration

The inspiration for this piece came from a painting I had made: French Farmhouse with Lavender Fields.

Initial design

The original image was quite a busy picture, so some windows and some trees have been omitted. This leaves a simpler composition but it will be enriched by the textured fabric.

Working design

Since the initial design was worked up on a grid, I felt there was no need to add one to this working design. The area to be sampled is already fairly complex, so the shapes it includes can be used to help get the relative positions correct.

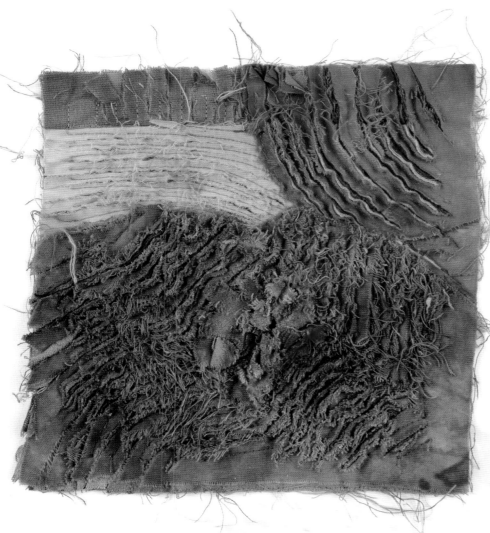

Creating a sample

I discovered from making this sample that I would need to sew the lines on the violet area and then cut away any excess fabric. The same applied to the green trees – all the slashing marks were sewn, and excess green fabric was then removed.

I also found that the slashing marks on the violet area needed to be bolder toward the front of the picture (i.e. the bottom) in order to create the right sense of perspective.

Sample taken from the detail opposite

Preparing the stack

Unlike *Sunset over the Sea*, this design used various bold blocks of colour with clear contrasts between one area and another. As a result, I decided to take a different approach by creating smaller separate stacks of colour that are combined on the base fabric. These are composed and worked before moving on to the next area.

1 Transfer the design onto fusible interfacing.

2 For the sky, lay a stack of five or six layered strips of different light blues in the sky area and tack into place. With a light blue bobbin, machine the parallel lines for the sky only. Turn the stack over and cut away all excess light blue.

3 Fill the lavender field area by laying a stack of five or six blue and violet strips in the area. Tack in place, match the bobbin thread and sew all the lines. Turn the stack over and cut away all excess blues and violets.

4 Repeat the method for the yellow area.

5 Slash between all the lines in the sky and lavender field areas.

6 Make a stack of three pink and beige fabrics for the house and tack this stack in place over the slashed sky area. Sew the outlines of the house and then cut away all the excess pink.

7 Make trees in the same way, using stacks of three green fabrics for each tree, and placing them over the slashed sky area.

8 The piece can now be finished as for a single stack work. Any remaining details such as doors and windows are added with thread, rather than slashing.

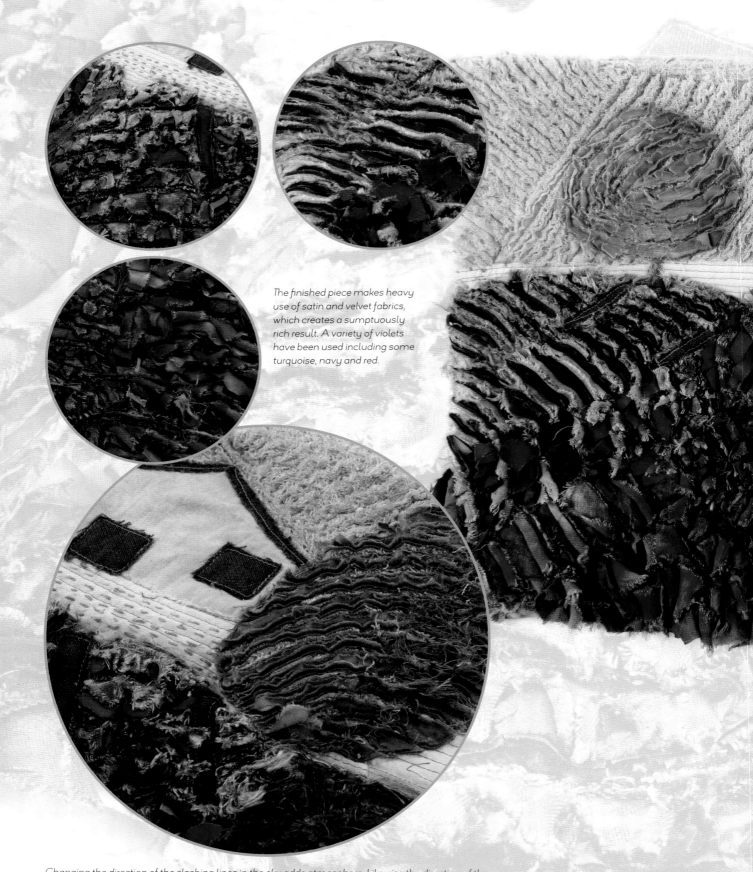

The finished piece makes heavy use of satin and velvet fabrics, which creates a sumptuously rich result. A variety of violets have been used including some turquoise, navy and red.

Changing the direction of the slashing lines in the sky adds atmosphere. Likewise the direction of the lines used on the trees has brought them to life. It is tempting to layer and slash all areas but leaving the building relatively unworked makes it a focal point on which to rest the eye.

The finished piece

Grasses in the Wind

By far the best way to record a scene is by sketching on location. It is an absolute joy to sit with a small chair and absorb and record what you see, feel, smell and hear. I have even been visited by a field mouse while sketching as well as numerous insects who are all quite brave when you sit quietly.

This little sketch was made using soft pastels. Although a messy medium, it allows you to work very directly with the paper, pushing and blending the colours together with your fingers.

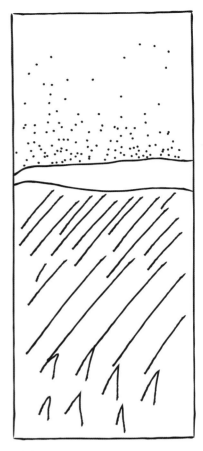

Original inspiration

A coloured sketch, made en plein air, of a field local to me. The grasses in the wind inspired me as they in themselves are layered, so they move just like the fabrics that I create. I begin to wonder if I draw like I stitch or stitch like I draw!

Initial design

The lines in the lower half suggest the prevailing movement of the grasses in the wind, while the smaller triangles at the very bottom add texture and interest, while helping to add depth and perspective to the scene.

Working design

This coloured, full-size working design shows a small area to sample (marked in red). Being too large for cartridge paper, the design has been worked on lining paper.

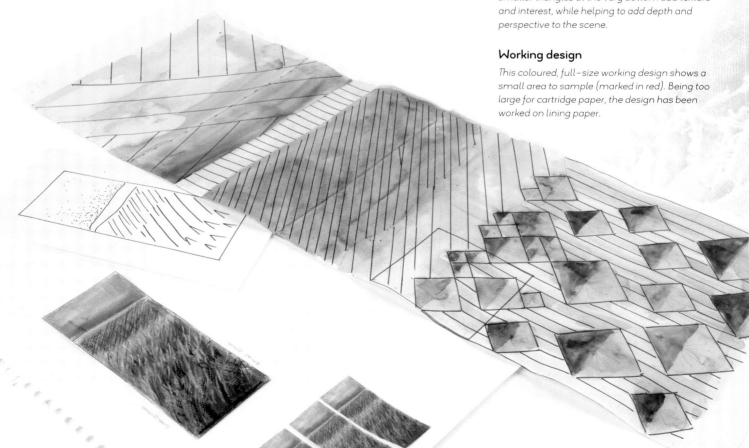

Creating a sample

Although there was not actually any red in the original drawing, layering my fabrics quickly revealed that the greens needed something to contrast with them, in order to make them more lively and vibrant. A strong warm orange-red, opposite green on the colour wheel (see page 76), proved an excellent contrast.

I discovered from this sample that some of the red fabric would need to be cut away and a few embroidery stitches would be needed to hold open some of the 'pockets' in order to help embellish the piece.

Sample taken from the detail opposite

Preparing the stack

As the top layer will be the most dominant, it is best to lay the fabrics to recreate the scene closely, remembering to overlap the bands of colour. Ensure that all areas are covered with at least five layers to ensure maximum freedom when slashing. If necessary, you can peel back a layer and add a few more beneath if you have a thin patch.

1 Trace the full working design onto a sheet of interfacing, drawing onto the glue side. Lay the interfacing down and begin to build up the layers of fabric on top of the glue.

2 Place the coloured full working design (see opposite) alongside the interfacing so that you have visual reference to work with.

3 Lay a stack of five or six light blue fabrics in the sky section, taking them just below the horizon so that they will blend into the yellow field below.

4 Build up layers for the green area, including some fabrics in bolder, contrasting colours and textures: glimpses of these will be revealed through the slashing. This is particularly important in the area where you are going to cut the large triangles. I used oranges in the sample piece above, and blue in the final piece (see overleaf).

5 Carefully tack all the layers in place before you machine the design.

73

The finished piece

Although I do like the finished piece it has come out somewhat darker than I had originally intended. However, as I have made the initial drawing I can go back at some time and creative another piece at the same size (and so re-use the design work) but changing the colours a little.

In the next piece, I might stick more closely to the original colours and another in monochrome using whites and creams. I could also change some of the slashing marks. This is the joy of the techniques: you might find making a piece encourages you to make another – or even a series.

Developing the design

This detail shows the initial sample placed on top of the finished piece. Note how the issues identified in making the sample (the over-dominant red of the pockets) have been altered for the final piece.

The triangles are held open with a few long stemmed French knots made using a complementary-coloured thread.

This detail shows how a layer of red 'sharpens up' the greens, giving a powerful vibrancy to the piece.

Very fine, narrow parallel lines were used in the sky to create interest without adding too much texture and complexity.

Creating with colour

We have covered a lot about achieving texture in layering fabrics. The other most important element is the use of colour. With layering, you need to consider not only the surface colour, but also the colours that lie beneath. The slashing will reveal these colours and appear to mix them together. This is much like mixing paint, and a lot that is applicable to your fabric art can be learned by playing with artists' paints.

This is how it works

With colours you can set a mood, attract attention, or make a statement. Colours affect us in numerous ways, both mentally and physically. A strong red colour has been shown to raise the blood pressure, while a blue colour has a calming effect. You can colour to energise, or to cool down. By selecting the right colour scheme, you can create an ambiance of elegance, warmth or tranquillity, or you can convey an image of playful youthfulness. Colour can be your most powerful design element if you learn to use it effectively.

The full colour wheel on this page can be used to work out relationships between colours, which can help you create striking combinations and effects when layering. The smaller colour wheels on the opposite page show wheels of the primary, secondary and tertiary colours in isolation.

The colour wheel

The colour wheel is a traditional way of showing colour relationships. Similar, or analogous, colours sit next to a colour, while complementary colours sit opposite each other. This is explained in more detail opposite.

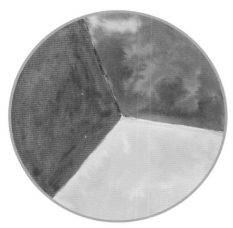

Primary colours

These are the colours that cannot be mixed from other colours: red, blue and yellow. They can, however, be combined to make useful ranges of colours – the secondaries and tertiaries.

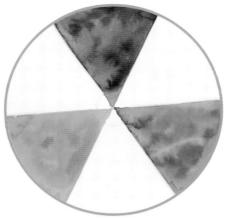

Secondary colours

These are the result of mixing two of the primary colours, resulting in orange (a mix of red and yellow), purple (a mix of red and blue) and green (a mix of yellow and blue).

Tertiary colours

Made by mixing two secondary colours together or by mixing a primary colour with the secondary colour closest to it. There are six tertiary colours: red–orange, yellow–orange, yellow–green, blue–green, blue–violet and red–violet. I like to call these fruity colours, as they include hues similar to limes, tangerines and berries.

Complementary colours

Complementary colours are pairs of colour that sit on opposite sides of the colour wheel: e.g. red is the complementary of green, yellow is the complementary of purple, and blue is the complementary of orange.

When mixed together physically, as in painting, complementary colours combine and cancel each other out. This means that they produce a grey colour that is neutral, like white or black. It is not possible to physically merge fabrics, but the principle can be applied through optical mixing.

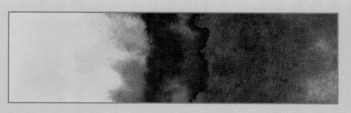

Physical mixing

Mixing complementary colours together will result in a neutral grey.

Optical mixing

When areas of paired complementary colours are placed next to each other they create the strongest contrast for those particular two colours, making both seem to sing out from the page. This is at the heart of optical or visual mixing, which is what makes the layering technique so effective: it allows you to put complementary colours next to one another for great vibrancy.

Optical mixing

Placing complementary colours next to one another will make both colours appear more vibrant. Note that placing equally wide stripes of complementary colours next to one another creates a balanced effect. This causes the colours to cancel each other out somewhat. Changing the proportion of the stripes – as in the lower example – will cause the colours to 'zing'!

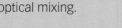

TIP

Due to this striking colour clash, the term 'opposite colours' is sometimes used rather than 'complementary colours'.

Layering with colour

I take a lot of inspiration from Vincent van Gogh (1853–1890). I am in awe of how he made colours 'zing' – with thoughtful placement of dashes of red paint, he sharpened the greens on his canvas. When he painted a face he used a lot of yellowish-orange for a skin colour, then added patches and shadows of blue. What he was doing is taking an analogous (closely related) group of colours, then placing a small amount of a complementary colour from the opposite side of the colour wheel to enliven the original colours. In the portrait example, the blue shadows complement the yellow-orange skin, making both appear more vibrant.

The artist Georges Seurat (1859–1891) used the technique of pointillism, a form of painting in which tiny dots of primary colours are used to generate the visual illusion of the presence of secondary colours, to similar effect.

Have a play with your paint to copy these great artists' techniques. These two techniques are very useful to bear in mind when layering, as the visual mixing gives lots of options without sacrificing vibrancy and brightness.

Opposite:
Wheatfield

Inspired by Vincent van Gogh's Wheatfield series of paintings, this fabric art piece reflects the colour and brushstrokes for which van Gogh was renowned. Leaf shapes with a few straight stitches depict the ears of corn whilst the curved slashing shows the stalks of the wheat bending in the wind. Have you spotted the bird in the top left corner? This was cut out and placed on the surface prior to the slashing.

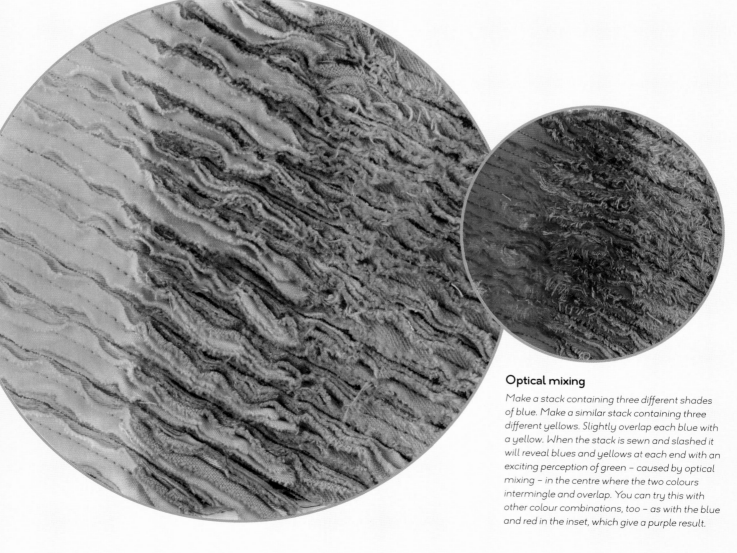

Optical mixing

Make a stack containing three different shades of blue. Make a similar stack containing three different yellows. Slightly overlap each blue with a yellow. When the stack is sewn and slashed it will reveal blues and yellows at each end with an exciting perception of green – caused by optical mixing – in the centre where the two colours intermingle and overlap. You can try this with other colour combinations, too – as with the blue and red in the inset, which give a purple result.

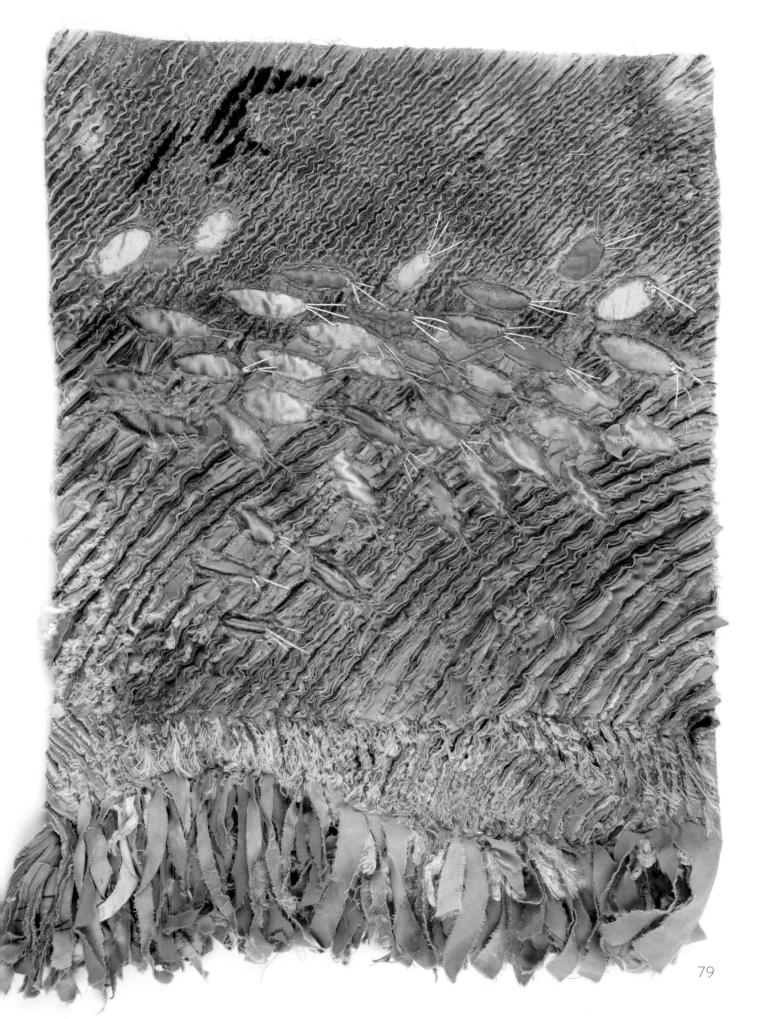

Other colour relationships

This page shows some other example schemes that you can use as a starting point for your own projects. The colours are shown as stripes, in case you want to try layering similarly-coloured fabrics in these orders. However, feel free to vary and experiment with the order.

Harmonious schemes tend to vary only a small amount from a single hue.

Harmonious colour scheme

In visual experience, harmony is something that is pleasing to the eye. It creates an inner sense of order and balance. When something is not harmonious, it is either chaotic or boring and bland.

As a rule, colours that are close to one another on the colour wheel are harmonious, as in the examples here.

Subtle schemes tend to favour soft pastels shades, and eschew high impact or contrasting colours.

Subtle colour scheme

These colours are not conspicuous. They can be described as shy and aiming to fit in, rather than shouting and competing for attention. A subtle colour scheme used with the layering techniques will give the texture more chance to excel and shine.

Amongst the most striking schemes are those that include a single accent colour alongside a number of harmonious colours. In each of these examples, four colours that are close to one another on the colour wheel form the basis, and a high contrast accent colour from the opposite side of the colour wheel is added to enliven the group. The proportions of the colours play an essential part of this scheme – if you use too much of the accent, you will lose the impact.

Accent colours

Accent colours are used to emphasis a colour scheme. They should be used sparingly. They work best when using a group of colours which are very close on the colour wheel and selecting an accent colour from the opposite side of the wheel. This accent will liven up a colour scheme.

It is a favourite scheme for interior designers: when designing a scheme, they might choose all the soft furnishing in subtle greens and then add a few subtle complmentatry touches through terracotta piping on a cushion, for example. It is a simple rule but works every time.

Colour sketches

Pink and blue are close to one another on the colour wheel and make for a harmonious combination, whatever the subject. These sketches show that particular colour combinations can be used effectively in almost any artwork – from sun–kissed fields to undersea denizens. Be inventive, and really look at what colours are present in your source material.

Analogous colours

The polychromatic little sample has colours arranged in analogous groups for maximum impact: groups of reds, plums and purple alongside a yellow, orange and lime group.

This sample has been cut with the design on the grain of the fabric which has allowed the fabric to fray. By placing the design on the bias they would not be fraying.

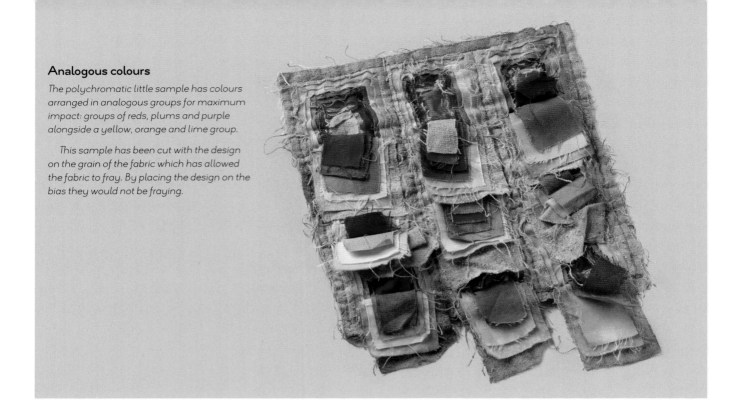

Accent colours

This is a test piece made as a sample for a large hanging of an herbaceous border. Lush greens portray the foliage with harmonious blue and violet flowers peeping through. The orange-stemmed French knots are used as a high-contrast accent colour that catches the eye and adds interest without dominating the piece entirely.

Sunset Trees

The trees are set in front of a dramatic sky displaying a complementary colour scheme of yellow and purple. Nature has a wonderful ability to shock us with its colour combinations.

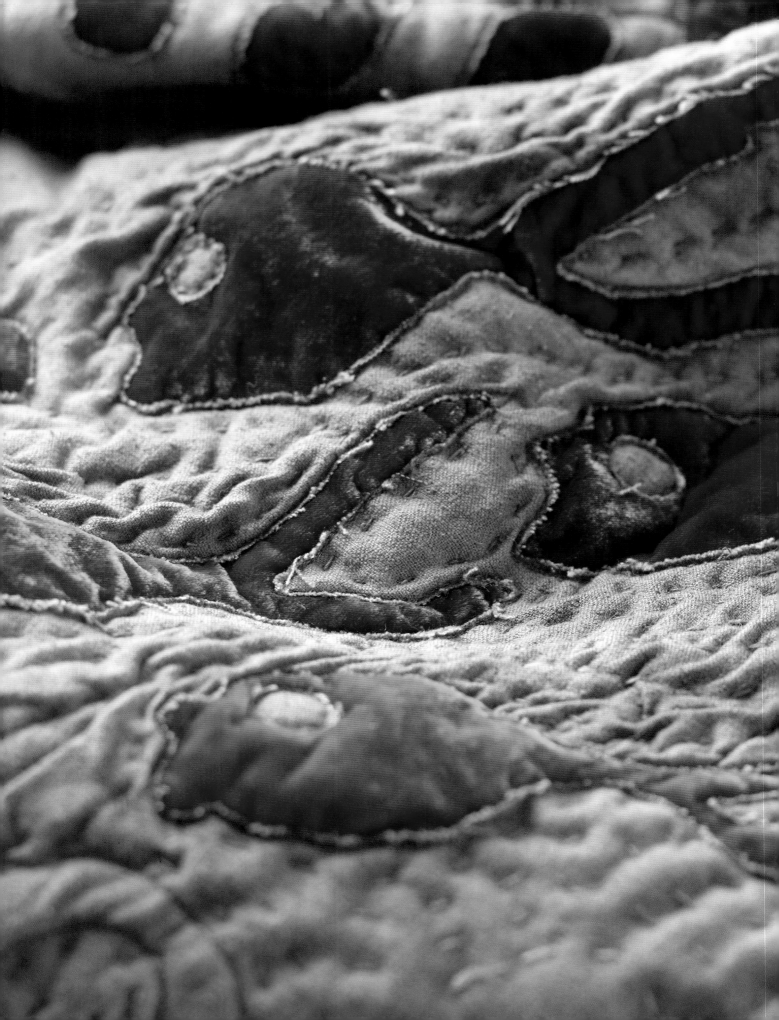

PUSHING THE BOUNDARIES:
ADVANCED TECHNIQUES

Trapunto

The word *trapunto* is Italian and means 'to quilt' or 'to embroider'. Trapunto is also sometimes called 'stuffed technique'. I use this technique to enhance my layered work. The layering and slashing techniques are shown to their best effect when the fabric is bent over, curved or and folded to catch the light and give it an extra dimension.

To produce a trapunto effect, the layered work is created and slashed with a very firm base layer. Small slits are made from the back and stuffing is placed into some areas to pad them out to achieve a raised effect on the front of the work. Once stuffed, the slit is sewn up just like a little operation scar. The firm base fabric forces the padded raised effect to fall to the front of the work.

Visual complexity
This detail shows leaf shapes with areas cut out. These allow the viewer to see the layers beneath, and creates the impression of a very intricate, involved piece. Note that the colour scheme is deliberately restricted to muted earth tones. This was both to evoke stonework, and to allow the texture to take centre stage.

Carving in architecture

Inspired by architectural carving, this piece is constructed of three layers: wool blanket, beige cotton and brown velvet. It is a perfect example of trapunto as the technique has been used extensively on the bottom layer to give a high relief to the border rope design.

The rope border was drawn on the reverse and machined before the large central section of cotton was cut away and slashes were made in the rope pattern. Small incisions were made from the back into the rope border channel which was then stuffed with polyester stuffing. This gave the rope a good rounded, raised effect and made the most of the slashes, opening them up as the fabric was stretched over the stuffing.

When finished the whole piece was backed with a heavy calico which further forced the relief to come to the front of the piece. Three-dimensional layers have been added on top to further increase the sense of depth and relief.

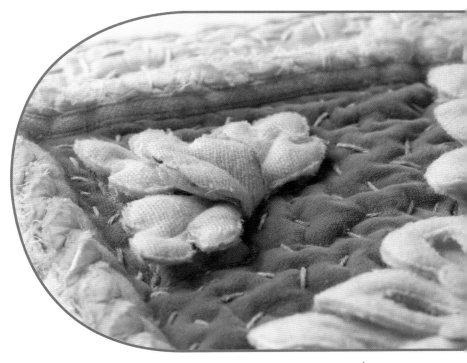

Layering
Here, a corner of the four-sided leaf motif has been folded over and secured to the centre to create yet another layer.

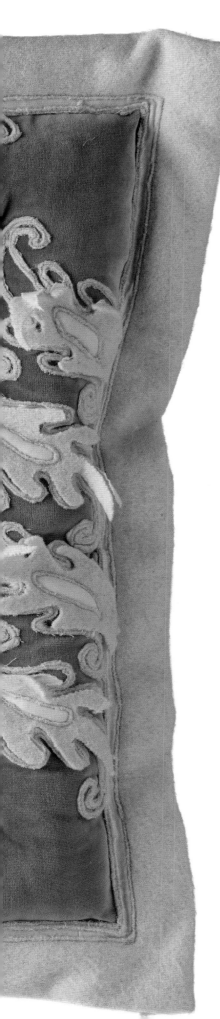

Angels in architecture

This example of the trapunto technique shows how multi-layered work, with areas stuffed to exaggerate the relief, can create great depth and structure.

As a frequent visitor to museums and historical buildings I have been struck by the magnificent work of Grinling Gibbons (1648–1721), one of the finest sculptors and wood carvers in England. The more I looked and the more drew, the more I found myself inspired by his exceptionally skilled work and wanted to see what I could achieve in my own chosen craft.

His fascinating work has provided me with inspiration for some considerable time, which has resulted in a body of work consisting of several panels. It is a source of inspiration that I hope to revisit and build upon.

Contours

The head is tucked beneath the wings. The heavy padding this technique creates allows you to produce very subtle contours.

Dimples

Tiny pin prick stitches have been added to create a dimpled effect on the wings – an approach that is only effective with thicker raised areas.

Double trapunto

This details shows double trapunto. Part of the top surface – the centre of the leaf – has been stuffed before being laid over another surface (the border) which is in turn stuffed again.

Multiple layering

Trapunto looks good when built up considerably. In this example, up to five layers are mounted onto the ground fabric.

Carved column

This 2m (6½ft) tall column is one of a pair made for a textile tableau entitled *Jabberwocky*, which was themed around the world of Lewis Carroll's book *Alice's Adventures in Wonderland* and its sequel, *Through the Looking-Glass, and What Alice Found There*. It is a great example of how trapunto can be used as an accenting technique, rather than being the dominant technique, as in the previous examples.

This column was created flat. A metal armature are been concealed in the bottom and top 25cm (10in) which holds the piece in shape, creating the illusion of the hollow half-pipe being a full column.

In addition to making extensive use of trapunto, this piece also demonstrates how effective repeated even slashing can be in creating texture. When working on a piece of this size, the scale of your work needs to be taken into account – you can afford to be very bold with the design elements.

The finished piece

Stuffing

The trapunto technique has been used here to give the hearts more form. They were stuffed from the back , as were the row of ovals. Trapunto is wonderful for adding a sense of dimensionality to your work, which is particularly important for large pieces – it is easy for more subtle textures to get lost from a distance.

Strapwork

The strapwork in this design has been stuffed from the back to allow it to stand proud of the surface.

Trapunto carving

As with the other pieces in this part of the book, the following piece was inspired by architectural carvings. Layering, slashing and stuffing are ideal techniques to create textile work that represents the very sculptural and three-dimensional work of stone- and woodcarvers.

The stuffed area will distort so it is advisable to use a fabric like wool or jersey (t-shirt fabric) which will 'give' a bit.

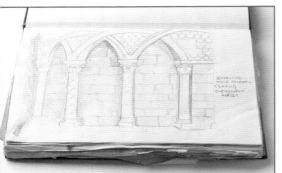

YOU WILL NEED

30cm (11¾in) squares of fabric in three harmonious tones: I used dark knitted blanket, mid-grey cotton, and off-white cotton

One 30cm (11¾in) square of opaque white backing fabric

One 30cm (11¾in) square of heavyweight calico

Black permanent marker

Polyester stuffing

Basic sewing kit

Sewing machine and thread to match fabric

Pen, pencil and paper

Scissors and shears

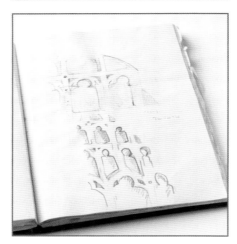

Inspiration

These sketches of architectural details informed and inspired the piece, though it is not based directly on any particular one.

Details of the finished piece

The finished piece

1 Use your inspirational images to draw your initial design on paper.

2 Develop the initial design into a full working design, as described on pages 50–55. The solid black lines here show where to machine. The red solid lines indicate where to sew after the backing calico is laid in place, while the broken red lines show where to cut prior to stuffing.

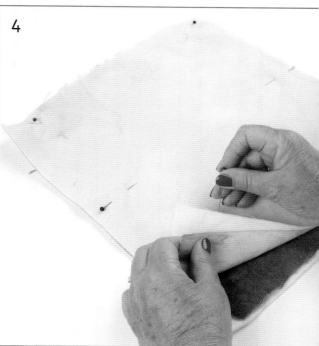

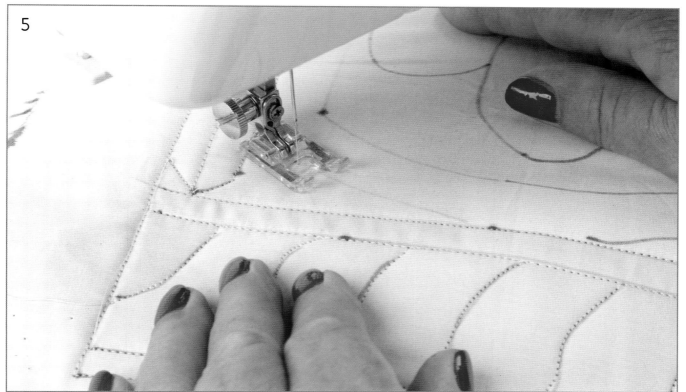

3 Trace the design onto white backing fabric using a black permanent marker.

4 Stack the dark blanket, mid-grey cotton and off-white cotton squares on top of the backing fabric, then pin all four layers together.

5 Working from the back, use your sewing machine with cream thread in the bobbin to sew along all the lines.

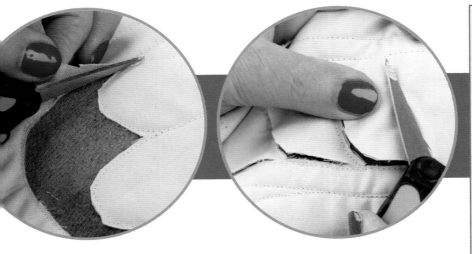

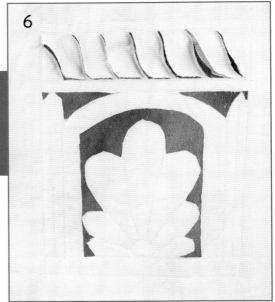

6 From the front, use fabric scissors to cut through the top two layers to reveal the dark blanket in the areas shown. Cut away the top layers entirely from around the fan area (leftmost image), but just make slits at the top (central image).

7 Cut down to the grey cotton at the borders as shown.

8 From the back, make incisions in the backing and dark blanket in the fan area.

TIP

You might find it helpful to mark the area with a pen before making the incisions.

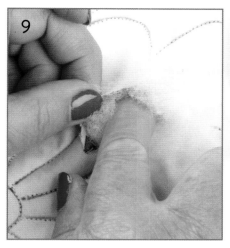

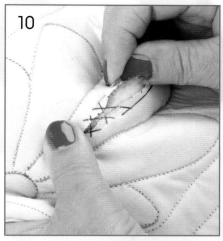

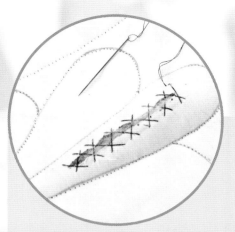

Herringbone stitch

A strong, useful stitch for sewing up slashes, herringbone stitch can be worked on either side of a cut as shown above.

To work it, follow the numbering of the diagram below, taking the needle alternately up and down through the fabric.

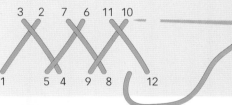

9 Stuff the individuals parts of the fan using polyester stuffing – do not over stuff, but add enough to create an obvious curve..

10 Sew up the incisions using a needle and strong thread to work herringbone stitch (see box, right).

11 Cover the whole of the stack at the back with heavy calico fabric. Working from the front, stitch through all the layers in the side of the arch, along the outer edges. Stitch above and below the rope area to stiffen this channel, then sew up the ends to finish. The inset shows the piece from the front.

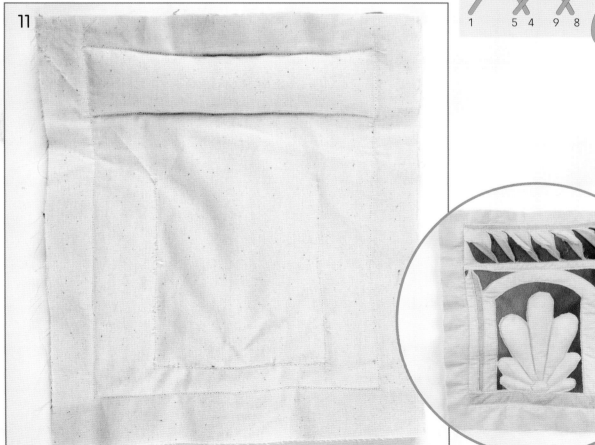

Book stacks

This technique emerged from my efforts to produce a really deep pile with the layering technique. I had been exploring a number of potential approaches to achieve this, but the inspiration for how the final technique works came from how books are manufactured. Rather than stacking all the pages in one go and then folding them in half, which would result in a thick, raised centre, books are made of multiple thinner sections: stacks of paper called 'signatures'. These sections are then folded separately, then grouped together to form the book.

I applied this concept to fabric, applying layers in small fabric 'book stacks'. I cut strips of fabric on the bias and stacked them four deep, then sewed down the centre to form the basic book stack. I sewed multiple book stacks very close to one another onto a sturdy base, which produced the thick deep texture for which I had been aiming.

My first attempts left lots of gaps and lots of frayed edges but also – as usual with experimentation – threw up lots more ideas for future projects. After a little refining, I was happy with the useful new technique I had developed.

Underwater creatures

Close inspection of a sea urchin reveals intricate patterns on the surface. By creating this pattern on a much larger scale, the complexity can really be appreciated and explored.

Designed to hang on a wall, this piece combines the book stack and trapunto techniques, and it measures 140 x 30cm (55 x 11¾in). A selection of thick and thin fabrics were used in the stacks, ranging from organdie to wool in various shades. The resulting piece of art is very weighty and is one of my favourite pieces.

Sea urchins provided inspiration

Padding and stitch detail

The centres have been stuffed from the back, painted with blue and brown dye and speckled with a scattering of small straight stitches.

The finished piece

Book stack detail

The book stacks in this piece are trimmed relatively short, which gives a particularly dense, neat and ordered appearance; perfect for representing the organic inspiration. Note the inclusion of peach and pale blue accent colours alongside the dominant ivory and cream.

Sculptural book stacks

Book stacks can be very versatile. While they work beautifully as part of a larger project, they also make interesting decorative objects in their own right. This project demonstrates three variations of the core method. Each of the techniques produces a slightly different type of richly textured pile and shows the beauty of repetition of simple shapes. Try all three and see which you prefer.

The first approach is the one with the broadest use beyond pure sculpture; and it is as shown earlier, with strips of fabric cut with the bias. The second is made in the same way, but using fabric strips cut with the grain. This approach produces a frayed edge. The third is simply a variation on the shape of the book: circles rather than rectangles.

I feel sure that with more experiments you will be able to come up with several more variations by changing the scale and types of fabric. They can be used as a surface texture, sewn directly onto a ground fabric, or, if the base fabric edge is cut and turned in, they can be used in a more sculptural fashion, as here.

YOU WILL NEED

125cm (49¼in) of cotton poplin or cotton organza

25cm (10in) heavy calico or similar strong fabric for base

Fusible interfacing

Pen, pencil and paper

Long ruler

Fabric marker

Teasel brush or dog grooming brush

Sewing machine and thread to match fabric

Zipper foot

Basic sewing kit

Scissors and shears

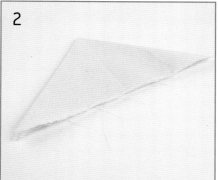

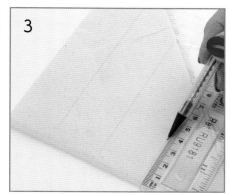

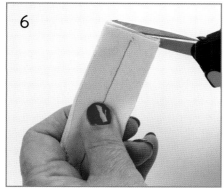

Bias book stacks

This is the basic technique, with the fabric cut on the bias.

1 Take a square of fabric and fold it in half diagonally.

2 Fold the resulting triangle in half and iron it flat. The fabric now has four layers.

3 Use a pencil to draw parallel lines spaced 3cm (1¼in) apart, along one of the folded edges.

4 Machine between each of the lines.

5 Use fabric scissors to cut along the pencilled lines, creating lots of bias strips. Depending on how long you want your book stack, you will need to make multiple copies.

6 Cut any folded edges.

7 Lightly trace the design onto your cotton poplin or organza, then place the fabric onto the heavy calico and tack together.

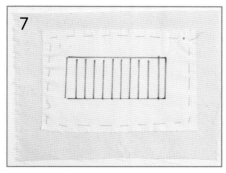

TIP
Remember to flip the design
over if it is asymmetrical.

8 Position one of the strips on the first line of your template.

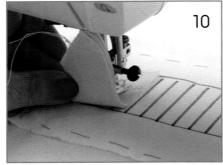

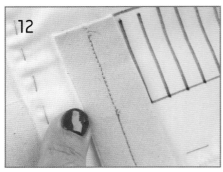

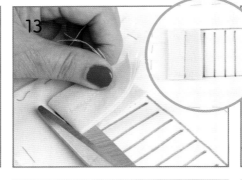

9 Secure the thread with a locking stitch, then work along the machined line.

10 As you approach the other side, pause and lift the strip to make sure that the stitched part just covers the line.

11 Fold the strip back down and mark the stopping point with a pencil.

12 Continue working to the pencil mark, then secure your thread.

13 Turn the excess strip back on itself, then trim it away carefully. This completes the first stack (see inset).

14 Change to a zipper foot on the machine. This will make it easier to work alongside the previous stack.

15 Fold the first stack on the piece over.

16 Place a second stack on the next template line along.

17 Machine the second stack into place as before, and trim.

18 Repeat all along the template.

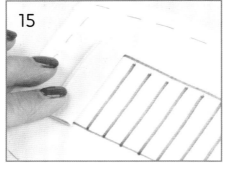

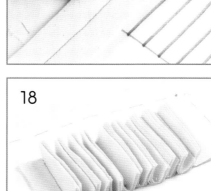

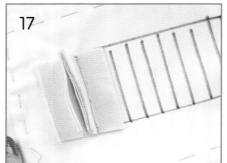

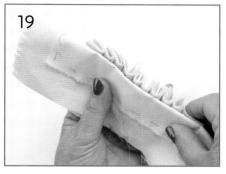

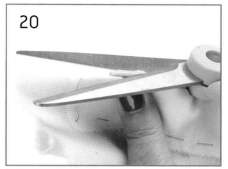

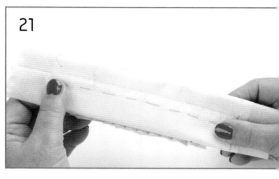

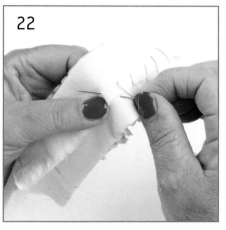

19 Fold the ending side of the piece under the stacks.

20 Carefully trim each stack in turn.

21 Fold the other side over the top of the ending side.

22 Secure it in place using slip stitch.

23 This completes the basic book stack. Rinse the piece under a tap and allow to dry, then brush it using a teasel brush to add texture and interest.

Try experimenting with different fabrics and lengths.

1

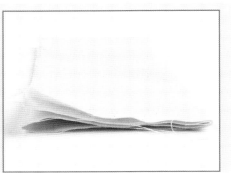

2

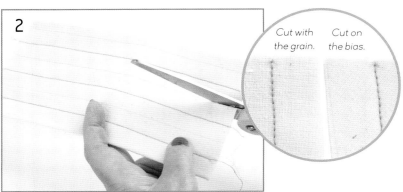

Cut with
the grain.

Cut on
the bias.

3

Fraying stacks

Almost identical in technique to bias book stacks, this approach will give a strikingly different result.

1 Fold the fabric in half, then half again, with the grain.

2 Working with the grain, mark and machine as for the bias strip stacks.

3 Assemble in the same way as the bias strip stacks, then use a teasel brush to fray the strip.

The completed fraying book stack.

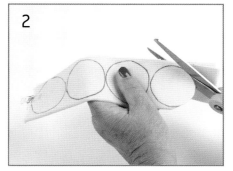

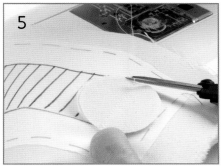

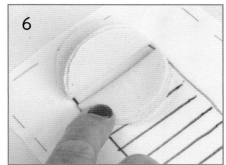

Circle stacks

Because the stacks for this technique are circular, folding with the grain or on the bias does not matter. However, folding as for the fraying strip stacks (see opposite) wastes less material.

1 Fold the fabric in half, then half again, to make 5cm (2in) wide strips. Draw round a 5cm (2in) diameter circle of card as many times as will fit between two folds.

2 Fold the fabric back up, secure the end, then cut just inside the circles.

3 Fold one stack of circles in half.

4 Lay the fold on the line of the template.

5 Unfold the circle stack, then machine it in place on the fabric along the crease using the zipper foot.

6 Fold the stack back and repeat with the next stack, placing it on the next template line along. Repeat to the end.

TIP

For a denser effect, abut the stacks to the previous stack, rather than working to the design lines.

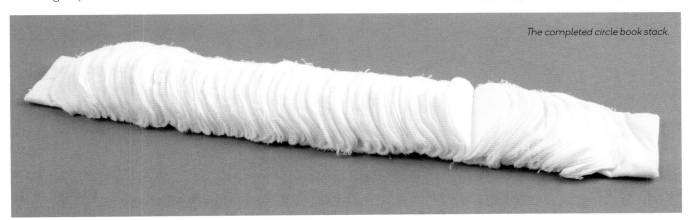

The completed circle book stack.

Working curves

The basic technique works very well for straight designs. It can also work for curved areas, but the following adjustments will make flowing curves much easier. The important part to remember when preparing your template is that the design lines (on which you stitch your stacks) must remain straight.

1 Attach the first stack, starting as close to the centre of the curved area as possible (rather than at one end).

2 Secure the next stack a little way away, rather than on the adjacent design line.

3 Gradually build up the design by filling in the gaps.

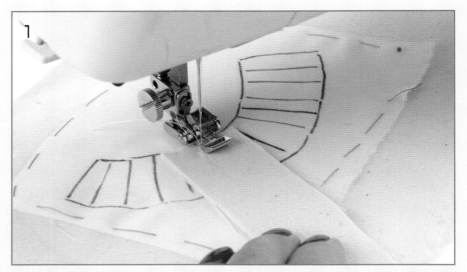

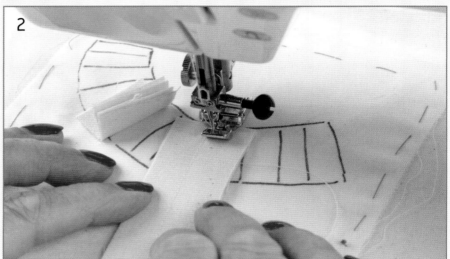

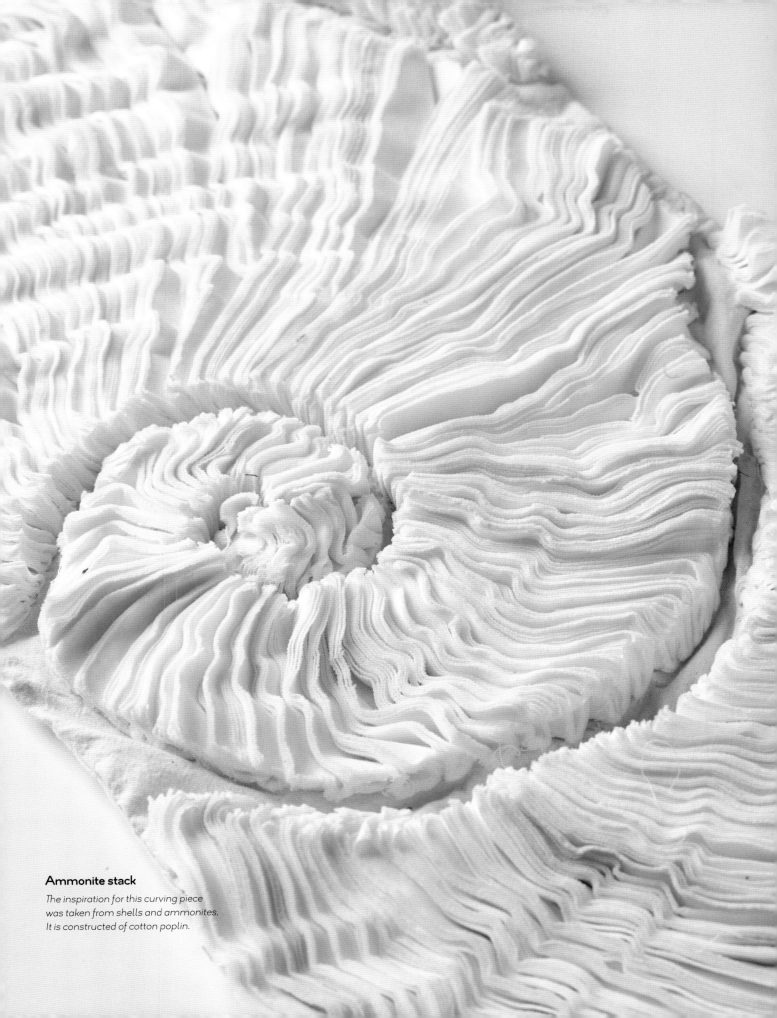

Ammonite stack

The inspiration for this curving piece was taken from shells and ammonites. It is constructed of cotton poplin.

Corals

Simple examples of the twisted spiral technique.

Twisted spirals

I discovered this technique whilst working with a shibori tie dye and found that it was very versatile as a manipulated fabric. It can represent many forms like flowers in bloom or in bud, funguses, small birds – even something as unusual as a unicorn horn.

Spiral samples

The technique is described in full on pages 116–121, but the heart of it is simply sewing along a spiral line and drawing the thread tight after every few stitches. The resulting textured fabric can be further manipulated into shapes and bundles. As shown opposite, the whole surface area can be textured using this simple spiral stitching.

Think about how you wish to use these spirals before you decide upon the fabric to use. The twisted spiral technique performs well in cotton poplin and would take on other forms in softer fabrics, like silk, or more ridged fabrics, such as wool blanket and felt.

It is important to use a strong matching coloured thread as all that tugging could cause it to break. If you run out of thread before the end of the spiral, you can simply fasten it off with a few stitches, then carry on with a new thread.

Corsage

This colourful corsage could alternatively be used as a curtain tassel or attached to a key to a cabinet. Each individual flower is made from a circle of fabric, the radius determining the length of the trumpet–like finished shapes. How tight you pull the thread will control the resulting shape of the trumpet.

Characterful birds

Each of these birds began life as a square of fabric. The beaks of these birds were made first, as small twisted spirals, which were fastened off then stuffed with a ball of polyester wadding. A circle of stitching was made to enclose the stuffing to construct the head before the remaining fabric was sewn into a bag shape. With the addition of swinging legs made from driftwood, they all come to life.

Each bird is made of a different sized and shaped piece of fabric, some of which are more oblong than square. When the fabric was wetted with a little PVA glue and water, it was possible to pull them into a variety of shapes giving them each an individual character.

Use of spirals

The beak spiral has a little brown dye painted on and two beady black eyes are attached above.

Finishing details

Small charms help to set off the wooden legs.

Short spirals

This little fellow is a baby with a short spiral beak.

Queen of Hearts cloak

This dramatic costume is an example of how the twisted spirals can be used as a supporting technique. I was looking for a way to produce a royal-looking ermine fur trim. Whatever your aim, there is usually a creative solution somewhere to be had.

The body of the cloak is decorated with parallel lines, made by slashing the surface fabric. Being black, the top layer remained over-dominant even once slashed, so I needed to remove the top black layer from every other channel to reveal more white.

The delicious red velvet hearts were stuffed from the back in trapunto style. The white pleated frill was soaked in tea to give it an antique look.

Use of spirals

Each little twist was fastened off and then dipped one by one into a pot of potassium permanganate. This turned them a deep purple temporarily, which gradually developed into a rich brown as the solution oxidised.

Combining techniques

The techniques combined very well. Note how the frill complements both the linear stripes and the dimensionality of the hearts.

Layering is very versatile – as it was extremely difficult to calculate how much fabric I would need for the cloak, I simply made batches and joined them all together.

Twisted blooms and buds

This project demonstrates both the basic principles and the versatility of the twisted spiral technique. Here, they are used to represent flowers in a collection suspended in the air – I took my inspiration from a similar installation piece of flowers and buds I had made as the centrepiece of an enchanted forest display.

Once you have learnt the basic technique, you can then let your imagination loose to see what else you can do with this adaptable shape. You might like to use a coloured fabric, or a plain one and dye it after it is complete. Different fabrics will give a completely different effect, though note that the fabric does need to be fairly soft to enable you to manipulate the stitching. The flowers and buds can be slightly stiffened with watered-down PVA glue.

Whether you make just one or two flowers to hang, or create an entire bunch, you will quickly learn just how versatile this technique can be.

YOU WILL NEED

44cm (17¼in) square of lightweight cotton

36cm (14¼in) square of lightweight cotton (for the bud)

4cm (1½in) radius circle of yellow-green fabric for the centre

Strong sewing thread

Small amount of polyester stuffing

PVA glue and brush (optional)

Pencil and ruler

Basic sewing kit

Scissors and shears

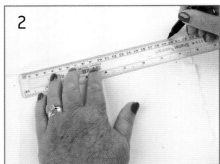

Twisted bloom

Petals

1 Take your large piece of fabric and fold it in half, then in half again.

2 Open out the fabric, measure 20cm (8in) outwards at several points from the centre, marking the fabric each time.

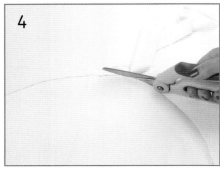

3 Join the dots with a pencil line.

4 Cut just along the inside of the line. You now have a circle of fabric.

5 Mark the centre of the circle with a light pencil dot.

6 Mark more dots, radiating outwards from the centre at a distance of 9cm (3½in). Join this circle of dots with a light pencil line.

7 Very lightly, use the pencil to draw a freehand spiral from the centre to the marks 9cm (3½in) out. Do not worry if the spiral is a bit wobbly.

8 Begin to sew along the spiral in small running stitches.

9 Begin at the centre and after about five stitches, pull the thread tight to gather the fabric. The thread needs to be strong so you could use it double or try using buttonhole thread.

TIP

When you run out of thread, sew a few stitches on top of one another to fasten off. Start again and carry on with a new thread.

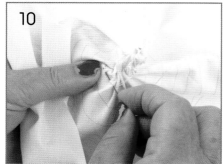

10 Continue working round the spiral in the same way.

11 When you reach the last outer line of the spiral, pull the thread to make sure the fabric is nicely scrunched. Fasten off really well with a few stitches

12 Roll the outside edge of the circle over between your thumb and first finger.

13 Over stitch this edge and pull the thread up slightly to encourage the edge to curl in and ripple a little.

14 Continue to work round the edge in the same way to gather the edge of the petals slightly.

The completed petals.

Flower centre

1 Take your small circle of coloured fabric and work some running stitches around the shape, approximately 1cm (½in) in from the edge. Pull up the thread until it forms a little ball shape.

2 Fill the piece with stuffing.

3 Pull up the threads tightly and fasten off. You will now have a small ball with a tail.

4 Poke the tail end of the flower centre into the flower shape as shown, then secure with a few stitches that are hidden in the folds of the fabric.

The bud

The bud is made in the same way as the petals, using the 36cm (14¼in) square of lightweight cotton and measuring 18cm (7in) outwards from the centre instead of 20cm (8in) at step 2. When gathering the edge (see steps 12–14), pull the thread until it forms a round ball-shaped bud.

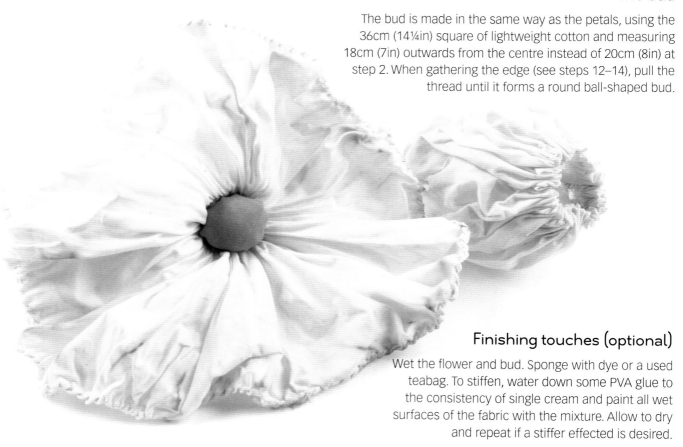

Finishing touches (optional)

Wet the flower and bud. Sponge with dye or a used teabag. To stiffen, water down some PVA glue to the consistency of single cream and paint all wet surfaces of the fabric with the mixture. Allow to dry and repeat if a stiffer effected is desired.

Hanging the twisted blooms

Sew a fine string to the pointed ends if you want them to dangle. I have used black thread here
– it is best to choose a colour of thread that matches where they are to hang.

Puffs

Suffolk puffs, also known as yo-yos after the children's toy, are simply a circle of fabric which is gathered around the edge so that it turns in on itself in a billowy fashion. Made from scraps of fabric, Suffolk puffs are neat at both the back and the front, making it unnecessary to line or back them when they are sewn together.

Suffolk puffs have a long history. references to 'puffs' appear as far back as 1601, when they were first used to adorn clothing and in quilt-making. The style enjoyed a resurgence in popularity in the 1920s, when puffs appeared on both clothing and furnishing.

My 'Essex puffs' are Suffolk puffs with attitude – they have a more blousy effect which is machined to a ground fabric. The resulting fabric is reversible, showing one side of raised round pillows and a reverse showing deep wells. This creates a new and exciting surface dimension, which pairs well with the textural and sculptural possibilities of layering.

Daisy Lawn

This hanging is based on Essex puffs in various sizes with small yellow stuffed Suffolk puffs attached to the centres. The centres have been offset for a more realistic flower look.

The whole hanging has been washed and the Essex puffs tugged to point in a downward direction – again, this helps them to appear more like real flowers.

Essex blues

The whole surface of this piece has been covered with Essex puffs. The reverse side of the puffs (see right) is just as attractive as the front, and reveals the edges of the inner circles. These have been machine stitched but they could equally well have been hand stitched. Each puff makes a little 'well', which is neatly framed by the base fabric.

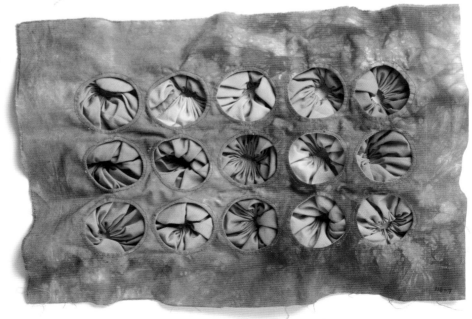

Using puffs

I love to use puffs – they are so versatile. Here are a few of my favourite ways to employ them in my work:

- Clusters of large and small, as in the examples on this page.
- Arranged in regimented rows.
- Made in a very soft silk, joined together and ironed flat.
- Made in a shiny fabric, placed on a contrasting matt ground fabric.
- Used alongside clusters of beads and buttons.
- As adornments on coat collars.
- As brooches.
- Made in cotton organdie and used as a lace curtain.

Orange puffs

After making careful observation of Black–Eyed Susan (Rudbeckia hirta) flowers, I recreated them with Essex puffs made from dyed cotton poplin. The centres are velvet traditional puffs in brown velvet and amber glass seed-beads.

White wall hanging

Similar to the wall hanging on page 122, this more subtle piece uses the same techniques for the cotton puffs, but is worked on a white cotton ground. The removal of the contrasting green background allows the texture of the puffs to become more important.

Opposite:
Essex puff hat
A very simple black hat is brought to life with the addition of richly coloured silk velvet puffs.

Flower puffs

Essex puffs can be used to interpret flowers, shells and pebbles or simply used in an abstract arrangement to create a breathtaking textured surface. This project gives stuffed velvet centres to three Essex puffs arranged on a space-dyed cotton fabric.

YOU WILL NEED

30 x 36cm (11¾ x 14¼in) piece of mottled green cotton poplin or similar fabric for the ground

30 x 36cm (11¾ x 14¼in) piece of white cotton poplin for the puffs

30cm (11¾in) square of silk/viscose velvet in yellow or brown

Pair of compasses

Lightweight card for templates

Hand embroidery thread

Polyester stuffing

Basic sewing kit

Sewing machine and thread to match fabric

Pencil and paper

Scissors and shears

These templates are provided at half of their actual size. You will need to scan or photocopy them at 200 per cent for the correct size.

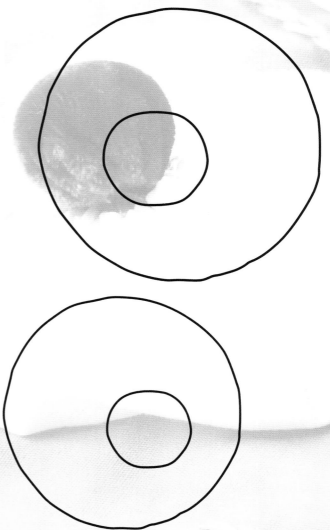

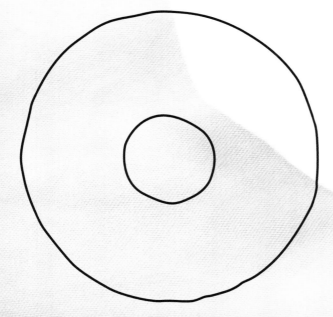

1 Use the template to cut out three card circles, then cut out the centre holes. Place the templates on the white fabric and draw around the outer edge and also the inner circle. Cut out the three white fabric circles just inside the outer edge of the drawn line, leaving the pencil line on the scrap fabric. Do not cut out the small inner circles.

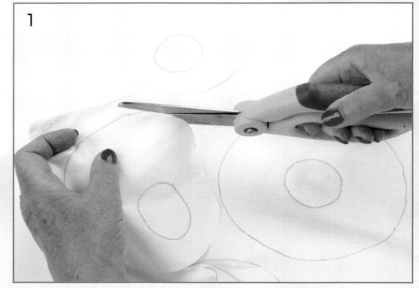

2 Place the three white circles on top of the green base fabric, overlapping them slightly to make a pleasing composition. Pin through the inner circle of each to attach them to the base fabric.

TIP

If you are using a printed fabric, arrange the circles on the wrong side at this stage.

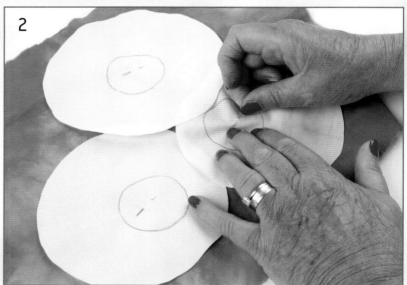

3 Thread the sewing machine with white thread at both top and bottom. Attach the three circles by sewing around each of the drawn small circles. Take care not to attach one circle to another and make sure that you sew complete circles.

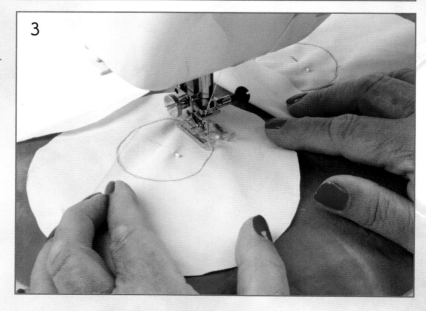

4 Cut out the three small centre circles, fairly close to the machine stitching but taking care not to cut the stitches. Cut through both the white and the green fabric.

5 Turn the white circles through the centre holes, turn the piece over and finger press the seams.

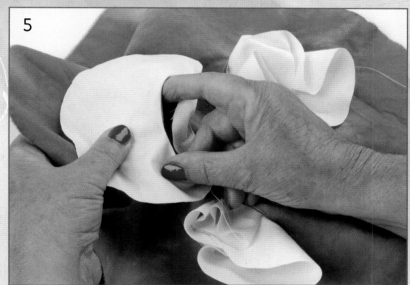

6 Turn the piece back over and sew machine lines close to the folded edge of the small apertures. This could be done by hand using a straight stitch or a chain stitch if preferred.

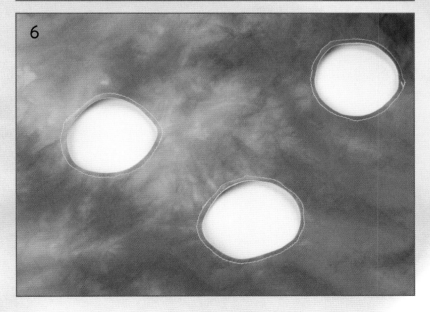

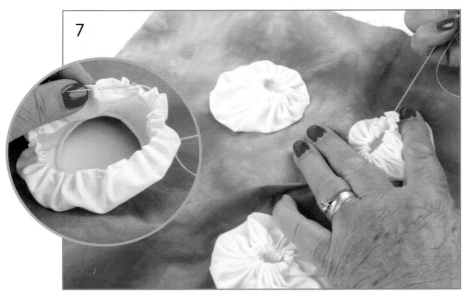

7 Turn in a 0.5cm (¼in) hem on each circle with a gathering running stitch, using a double length of cotton thread (see inset). Pull the thread tight to gather up the circle and secure with a few small stitches.

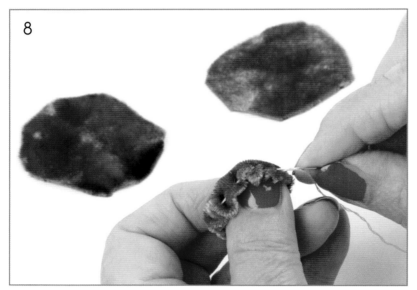

8 Cut three 5cm (2in) circles from the velvet fabric. Roll the edge of the circle and use a needle and yellow variegated thread to secure it with a running/gathering stitch.

9 Lightly pull the gathering thread to create a velvet ball. Fill with polyester stuffing. Close the ball with a few stitches to secure.

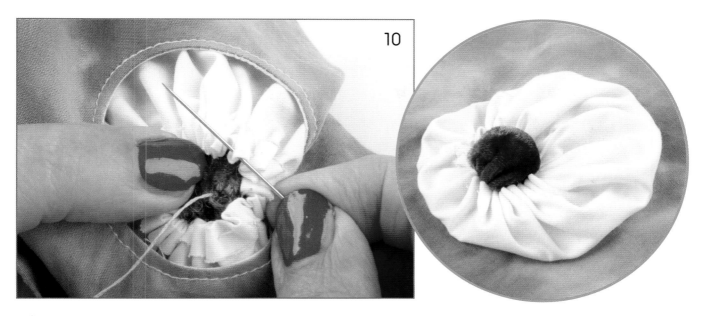

10 Place the velvet ball into the puff aperture. From the back secure the ball to the puff. Work small stitches around the ball until secure. This completes one Essex puff (see inset). Complete the others in the same way.

11 Lightly draw some scrolling guide lines around the puffs on the green base fabric then work chain stitch over the pencil line. Select an embroidery thread of a colour that blends rather than dominates.

TIP

Other line stitches can be used such as rope stitch or stem stitch.

THREE-DIMENSIONAL
APPLIQUÉ
PROJECTS

Handbag

For this handbag, carefully consider which fabric to choose. I would suggest quite a sturdy one for the outside. I have used cotton velvet, a thin layer of cotton poplin for the middle and a heavyweight knitted polyester for the base. You could also choose a different surface design from this book for a very individual look.

My favourite part of this design is the crocodile-skin like texture on the strap. It is effective on items that are curved or stuffed like a cushion.

For a larger tote bag, simply change the dimensions.

YOU WILL NEED

FRONT AND BACK:

Six pieces of fabric, each cut 4cm (1½in) larger than the front/back template (see opposite): two in green for the outside layer; two in yellow for the middle layer; and two in sturdy purple fabric for the base layer

STRAP

Three pieces of fabric in green, yellow, and purple cut 4cm (1½in) larger than the strap (see page 137)

One piece of interfacing cut 4cm (1½in) larger than the strap

Wadding the same size as the strap

Roll of heavy duty lining paper

Masking tape

Blue, red and black permanent felt tip markers

Basic sewing kit

Strong thread for sewing the strap

Sewing machine and thread to match fabric

Pencil and paper

Scissors, seam ripper and shears

The addition of a small flower – made using the twisted spiral technique (see pages 116–121) – helps to set off this attractive handbag.

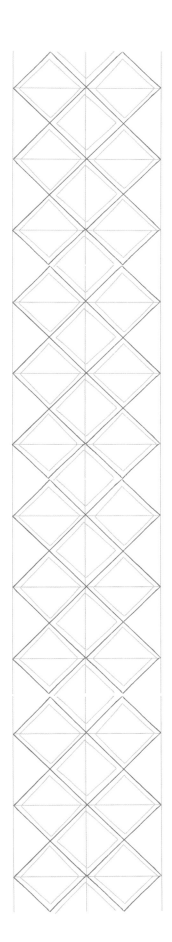

Strap template

This template is provided at half actual size. You will need to enlarge it by 200 per cent on a scanner or photocopier for the correct size. In addition, note that this represents only quarter of the length of the finished strap. You will need to copy the template on to lining paper repeatedly as described in step 7 on page 137. The full strap should measure 100cm (39in).

Front/back template

This template is provided at half actual size. You will need to enlarge it by 200 per cent on a scanner or photocopier for the correct size.

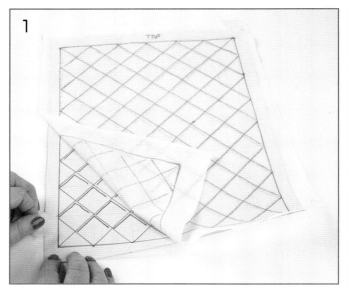

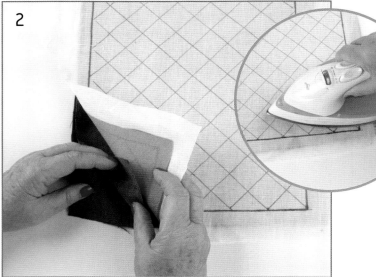

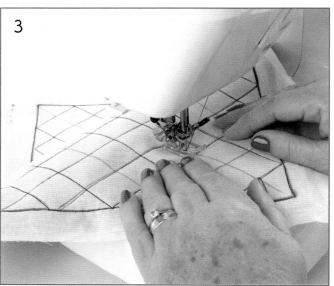

1 Transfer the template for the back/front onto good-quality wallpaper lining paper to the dimensions given and mark the top edge of the bag. Cut out the paper pattern and stick each corner to the table with masking tape. Lay the fusible interfacing on the patterns and trace the blue and black lines of the design template. Use masking tape at the corners to hold the interfacing in place.

2 Lay out the stacks for the front by laying down green, purple and yellow fabrics. The green fabric will be outermost, so keep it at the bottom. Place the marked interfacing (glue side down) on the top of the stack and iron on.

3 Match the bobbin thread to the outer fabric and sew along all the blue lines on the front and back panels.

4 Turn the piece over and use sharp scissors to cut through the green and purple layers of fabric where indicated in red on the template.

5

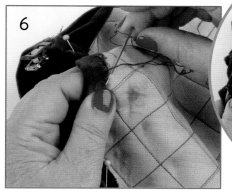

6

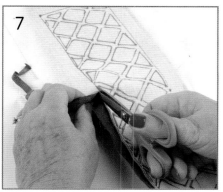

7

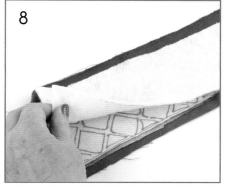

8

9

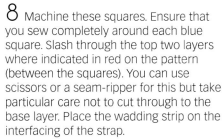

10

11

5 Cut away any excess cloth from the panel sides except for the front layer.

6 Repeat steps 1–5 for the back, then place the front and back right sides together and sew together at the sides and bottom using a 1.5cm (½in) seam allowance. Turn over the top edges of the panel towards the inside (i.e. the lining), pin, and secure with neat stitching. Wash and bloom (see inset).

7 Repeat steps 1–5 for the strap using the strap template. Copy the strap template onto the lining paper a number of times in order to achieve the correct length of 100cm (39in). Note that the blue lines are different on the strap: they are small individual squares rather than a connected grid. Trim away the excess seam allowance from all the layers apart from the top fabric.

8 Machine these squares. Ensure that you sew completely around each blue square. Slash through the top two layers where indicated in red on the pattern (between the squares). You can use scissors or a seam-ripper for this but take particular care not to cut through to the base layer. Place the wadding strip on the interfacing of the strap.

9 Tack the interfacing to secure it to the layers, then fold over the seam allowance of the long edges and ends. Tack to hold.

10 Fold the strap over in half lengthwise and tack together. Sew the ends of the strap, then hand stitch the two long sides together neatly.

11 Flatten the strap so that the hand-sewn seam is in the centre, then attach the strap to the side seams using a strong thread and taking the stitches right through to the inside of the bag.

Brooches

Jewellery does not need to be dominated by gems or precious metals like gold and silver. Textile jewellery is a fashionable alternative with many benefits: it is lightweight, tactile and needs no special equipment to make yourself. Using brightly coloured fabric will give a great effect, but you will need to make sure that the fabric is well rinsed and colourfast so that the dye will not rub or run off on your garments when being worn.

YOU WILL NEED

20cm (8in) circle of light green poly-cotton or similar fabric

15cm (6in) squares of fabric in the following colours: dark green, deep purple, mid purple, light purple, and yellow

Sewing machine and thread to match fabric

Scrap of polyester stuffing

Pencil and paper

Scissors and shears

Pair of compasses

Basic sewing kit

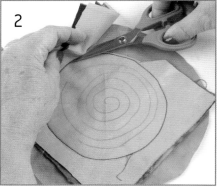
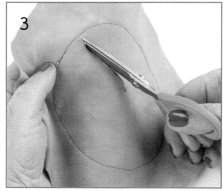

1 Stack the small squares. Start with the dark green square, then place the three purple squares on top, and finally the yellow square. Pin the stack of 15cm (6in) squares in the centre of the larger light green circle, then use a pair of compasses and an HB pencil to draw a 12cm (4¾in) diameter circle on the stack. Draw a freehand spiral from the centre of the yellow square out to the edge.

2 Machine stitch around the circle, then use scissors to cut away excess fabric from the outside of the circle, leaving the light green back fabric intact. This leaves you with a stack of circles attached to a larger green circle.

3 Turn over to the light green side and, cut a straight line outwards from the centre to the edge. Cut through the top five layers one by one, leaving the yellow layer uncut.

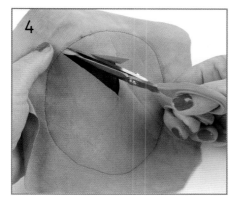
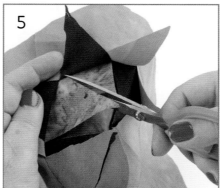
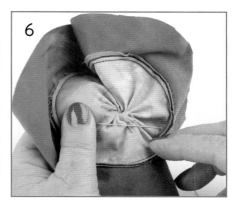

4 Starting from the centre again, cut another line outwards to the edge, a little further along, to make a flap.

5 Work around the circle in this way until you have created a star effect.

6 Turn the piece over. Use a needle and thread to work gathering running stitches along the spiral on the yellow fabric until the fabric gathers. It may not be necessary to sew the entire spiral.

7 Once you have worked to the outside of the spiral, pull up the thread to gather the fabric slightly on the front. Fasten off.

8 Run a gathering thread on the back around the machined circle.

9 Pop a small ball of polyester stuffing on top of the yellow spiral and pull up the thread to make the aperture about 5cm (2in) in diameter.

10 Turn under the outer edge of the light green with a gathering running stitch.

11 Use a small offcut of spare fabric to cover the stuffing (see inset), then pull the thread to close over the stuffing. Add a brooch back jewellery finding to finish.

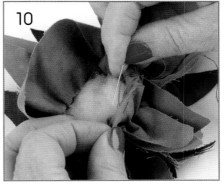

The finished brooch.

Scarf

This method makes a warm and stretchy textile that can be worn as a scarf. It can be made of new white t-shirt fabric – so you can dye it yourself – or, if you like the idea of recycling, you can make it from old garments made of jersey fabric. You might like to try an alternative fabric but it needs to be soft and non-fray or it will shed fluff every time you wear it.

The important part is not to skimp on the length. If you are to make a beautiful scarf you need to make one that is long enough to wind around the neck and still have enough hanging freely to show off your handiwork!

YOU WILL NEED

Five 180 x 21cm (70¾ x 8¼in) pieces of jersey (t-shirt fabric) in your choice of colours

Long ruler

Fabric marker

Sewing machine and thread to match fabric

Scissors and shears

Basic sewing kit

1 Stack the five long pieces of fabric on top of each other. Pin or clip at intervals to hold them in place, then use the pencil to draw a grid of 3cm (1¼in) squares on the top layer of fabric.

2 Machine this grid through all the layers, starting with the lines that run the length of the scarf. This will make it easier to machine the lines that run across.

3 Cut a cross on the centre of each square. Cut through all the layers but be careful not to cut through the lines of stitching. Wash to fluff up.

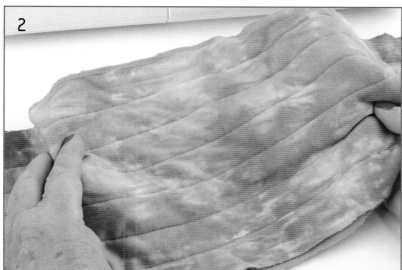

TIP

If you use recycled fabric you may need to join pieces together. To do so, butt the edges of one piece against another and join with a three-step zig-zag stitch, matching the thread to the fabric as closely as possible – this example is in a contrasting colour to help highlight the technique.

Going further

Having worked your way through all the techniques, you will have started to develop a comprehensive portfolio of ideas and skills to use in your textile artwork. You can now look back through this book and see how you could combine and take these ideas further.

You might push the boundaries of what you have attempted before, and to incorporate the techniques into your existing ideas and themes. For example, I have recently begun working with rust effects and have found that this combines beautifully with the book stacks in particular. My success with incorporating rust into my artwork has encouraged me to try other metallic effects in my work and I also intend to take the sculptural elements further to see just what I can do with these fascinating, versatile materials. Watch this space!

However, there is no need to go completely experimental. Perhaps your interest lies in more conventional patchwork. You can certainly incorporate small elements from this book into your work to give it a more contemporary edge without completely jumping into the *avant garde*.

Most of my work is quite large. I find working on such a scale is a good way to begin exploring these techniques, but you might equally well enjoy the challenge of making your work miniature – see just how far you can translate the pictorial scenes by exchanging rougher fabric and bold details for delicate fine cloth and small intricate stitches.

Clothing is another area into which these techniques would translate well. The book stacks remind me of fur and would make good trims and edges and terrific theatre costumes – Oops! I'm back into theatre costume which is where I began in my introduction. Writing this book has been a great journey for me and I hope you enjoy it as much as I have.

Happy experimenting!

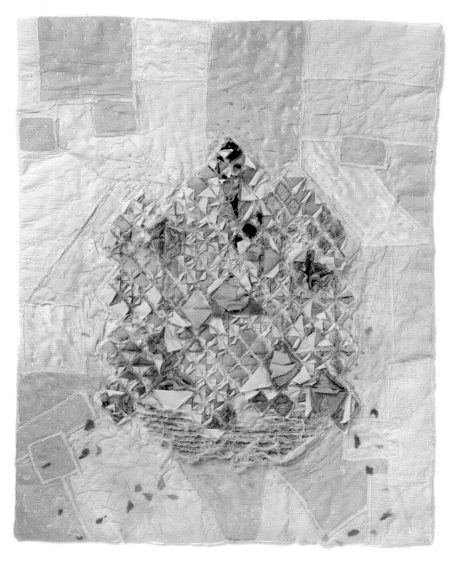

A bowl of flowers

Inspiration comes from many sources. The idea for this piece came when I was looking in a window of a gallery and saw a painting that I loved of a bowl of flowers painted in thick splodged paint. I particularly liked the background of very textured whites and creams, and decided to make my own interpretation using my own preferred medium – textiles.

Escape

I have begun a new body of work which reflects the fact that I am now spending some of my time in London. No pretty landscapes here but interesting nooks and crannies of a more industrial nature, allowing me to experiment with rusty book stacks, a darker palette and a more edgy design.

Index

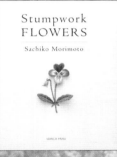

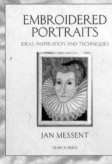

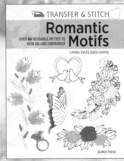

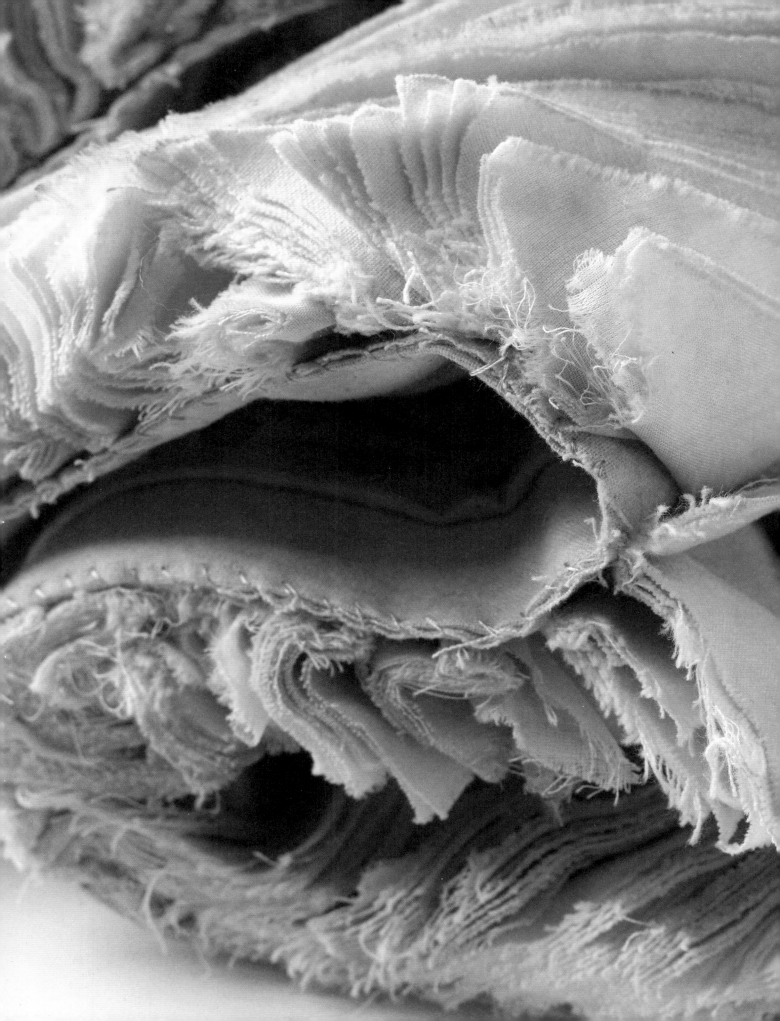